Dying Without God

T0058322

Dying Without God

François Mitterrand's Meditations
on Living and Dying

Franz-Olivier Giesbert

Introduction by
William Styron

Translated from the French by
Richard Seaver

Helios
press

Originally published in France under the title *Le Vieil Homme et la Mort*

Helios Press books may be purchased in bulk at special discounts for sales promotion, corporate gifts, fund-raising, or educational purposes. Special editions can also be created to specifications. For details, contact the Special Sales Department, Helios Press, 307 West 36th Street, 11th Floor, New York, NY 10018 or helios@skyhorsepublishing.com.

Helios Press® is a registered trademark of Skyhorse Publishing, Inc.®, a Delaware corporation.

Visit our website at www.skyhorsepublishing.com.com.

10 9 8 7 6 5 4 3 2 1

Library of Congress Cataloging-in-Publication Data is available on file.

ISBN: 978-1-61145-770-4

Printed in China

For me, the obsession with death has nothing to do with a fear of death.

—E. M. CIORAN

The fear of death is virtually meaningless. We need to have the humility to know that, in death, we're in the company of countless others, and that death is the only certain destiny that awaits us all. I'm not overly preoccupied with death but rather by the enormous question mark it represents. Is it nothingness? That's possible. If it's not, then what a great adventure lies ahead.

—FRANÇOIS MITTERRAND

One autumn morning, as he was coming back from a walk, he felt Death lay a finger on a particular point of his stomach; Death pressed, and it hurt. . . . His first reaction was one of violent fear, but at the same time a voice within him cried out, "At last!"

He was a somewhat solemn man, who loved books and who, until now, had thought he was inured to suffering, but when he was faced with it he found that he was as hapless as a child. He knew full well that Death had to come and he had prepared a place in his life for it. Now that it was ensconced there, he forgot his maxims, his resolutions, and he realized that from this moment on to live was to learn how not to moan.

—JULIEN GREEN,
THE VISIONARY

One day man enters old age as he would a large empty apartment at dusk. Through the window, he sees life passing by below, life enlarged by his memories and dreams, but henceforth he sees life only through that improbable and ghostly window. Then he too fades away and disguises himself as memory.

—ALEXANDRE VIALETTE,
NO H IN NATALIE

INTRODUCTION

$\mathcal{F}$RANZ-OLIVIER GIESBERT'S ELOQUENT and moving chronicle of a great man facing death inevitably recalled to mind my own first encounter with François Mitterrand on a splendid day in May 1981, when he was refulgent with life and embarking upon his presidency. I was one of a handful of foreign writers — Arthur Miller and Carlos Fuentes were among the others — invited to Mitterrand's inaugural, and on the trip to Paris by Concorde I had been bemused by an article in *Time* that, among other personal details, alluded to the president-elect's indifference to the pleasures of the table. As has been so often the case, *Time* was off target. Sitting opposite Mitterrand at the Elysée during the first lunch of his presidency, I thought I had rarely seen a man in such pleasurable thrall to a meal, digging into the foie gras from his native Landes with obvious zest and plainly relishing the *belles d'Argenteuil* spears of voluptuous white asparagus that he conveyed to his mouth with his fingers. The menu I've kept from that day indicates that one of the wines was a Château Talbot 1970, a great vintage that may have accounted for the flush on his face, although it was also plainly the flush of triumph. Fuentes, who had served as Mexico's ambassador to France and had been a friend and neighbor of the president, asked him how it felt to have won the prize. Mitterrand's response was almost boyish as he shook his head and exclaimed, "I still can't believe it!"

The glow I felt that day, which I shared with the other

writers, may have been connected with the impulse to look up to a leader for whom culture was an essential need. On a January day earlier in the year, Ronald Reagan had had his day of triumph, causing heartbreak and desolation among many of those who considered themselves civilized. Franz-Olivier Giesbert reports that years later Mitterrand's judgment upon Reagan was scathing: "The man was a nonentity. A complete nonentity." At the Elysée lunch the new president had not as yet met Reagan, whom he would regard as a "dullard." Yet he may have been reflecting a chagrin commonly felt among intellectuals everywhere when he asked me, with a touch of amusement, "How is it that your countrymen elected a master of ceremonies for president?" He said he'd seen a photograph of Reagan on a nightclub stage, introducing showgirls. This may have been impolitic of Mitterrand, placing me on the defensive, but I merely replied, "Americans have always wanted a master of ceremonies in the White House." Neither Arthur Miller nor I, nor, to the best of my knowledge, any other writer had attended the Reagan inaugural, which had been crowded with entertainment figures and business tycoons. How incongruous it was, I thought, yet how heady, to be seated near a French president who had surrounded himself so enjoyably with writers. And, as if to emphasize his concern for literature, he told Fuentes, who had inquired about his forthcoming agenda, that his first official act would be to grant French citizenship to two exiled novelists, the Czech-born Milan Kundera and Julio Cortázar of Argentina. Which in fact he did, that same afternoon.

I saw Mitterrand a number of times during his tenure, and always felt flattered and invigorated by the warmth of his greeting. Like most people I had no inkling of his illness, though the pain that Giesbert so harrowingly records during his last days must have already begun its inroads whenever I met him. He was always self-contained, imperturbable. And, bearing out the rather wistful yearning he expressed to Giesbert — "I would have liked to be a writer" — he spoke to me mostly of books and was endlessly inquisitive about the writing process. A year or so after the inaugural, when I was in Paris, he asked Norman Mailer and me to a small dinner at Le Train Bleu restaurant in the Gare de Lyon. A remark Mitterrand made to Giesbert concerning the best way to travel during political campaigns reminded me of my conversation with the president. "Always remember to take along a book," he said, and one of the books he told me he had been immersed in during his campaign travels was the translation of *Sophie's Choice*. He asked me numerous questions about the way I had put the book together — he seemed fascinated by the autobiographical aspects of the story, and by the research I had done in Poland — and our chat about my work continued for much of the meal until at last our attention turned to Mailer, who caused Mitterrand considerable merriment with his scheme to circumvent warfare: rent a remote island and there compel the leaders of the contending nations to hold a tourney, a joust, and work off their enmity like medieval knights.

I dined with Mitterrand on several occasions after that during his presidency: at the Elysée again, with Milan Kundera, and once memorably at the Reagan White House, of all places, where amid a throng of CEOs and Republican senators I found myself seated (at his behest, I'm sure) not at some far satellite table but directly to his right, a placement that allowed us, after an exchange of knowing and conspirational looks, to talk all evening about Thomas Mann, Camus, and Victor Hugo. Giesbert tells us that Mitterrand had small acquaintance with American literature, and came to it late in life, and I'm sure this is true; still, I was touched to read in a clipping from *Le Monde* that during his final vacation he took along my book of stories, *A Tidewater Morning.*

My encounters with François Mitterrand, while poignant and meaningful to me, had a certain superficiality, partly because my French is only, as they say, serviceable, and our usually public settings never really provided the relaxation for a truly extended talk together. I could never remotely claim to having got to know the man. Nor did I perceive that malign aspect that caused so many people, apparently with justification, to hate him. In addition to the biting intimacy Giesbert brings to his subject — a canny understanding drawn from long friendship, along with a lucid objectivity that derives, by the author's own admission, from love and hate in equipoise — there is a powerful fascination in this portrait of a soul floundering bravely deathward. It is not often that we are offered page after page of an historic figure in the process of physical dissolution, and Giesbert's focused depiction is both compassionate and oddly ruthless. We see the unkempt, even slovenly Mitterrand, industriously picking his teeth; although the dental detail makes the reader wince, it seems somehow necessary, given the author's obvious determination to spare nothing in his trompe-l'oeil close-up.

On a purely physical level, what makes this narrative

so fresh and appealing is Giesbert's gift of observation; his eye for detail is that of a good novelist. An episode with a bothersome fly, flitting between the author and Mitterrand as they discourse seriously about socialism, has both the saving grace of humor (a mood that often lights up these pages) and a more sinister symbolism, as if the fly represents the crowd of buzzing vexations that had beset the president's immediate past, as well as the ultimate vexation of death itself. Much of this book is about the raw fact of suffering. Death is an almost smothering presence as we track Giesbert and Mitterrand, "enveloped in his pallid shroud of flesh," yet a constant wonder is the president's mysterious renewal of energy, which, transcending awful pain, keeps him talking and provides a kind of unflaggingly fascinating libretto to this final act.

The talk is sharp and varied. Napoleon. Clemenceau. Socialism. Gorbachev. The brief shelf-life of politicians. Chirac and Jospin — he likes both. And of course, there is the matter of women. Vast numbers of Americans, for whom sex possesses more than a touch of the diabolical, were shocked to discover, as the word leaked out over the years, that the president of France had not only numerous girlfriends but a mistress by whom he had fathered a child. Yielding "to some kind of carnal temptation," Mitterrand tells Giesbert, "in itself is reason enough to govern." So: more shock for our countrymen who still pretend to believe that men want to be president in order to balance the budget. Of course, there are exceptions, and a French exception would have been de Gaulle, who, to the best of Mitterrand's knowledge, sought "no straying from the straight and narrow." Wonderfully, Mitterrand elaborates by pointing out that "de Gaulle wasn't a man. He was an idea. He was France incarnate, and France couldn't be laid."

In the same vein, Mitterrand had affectionate feelings for President Clinton, and tells Giesbert that he is fascinated by his "animality," which probably is a polite term for something steamier. Giesbert has a long and colorful passage about Mitterrand's passion for women, his predatory ways, his patient seductions, his genuine love for members of the opposite sex, who "were the only beings on the face of the earth capable of making him abandon his cynicism." A glimpse of this avid lover, whom Giesbert recalls from the old days — when he would meet him in the morning, resembling "not so much a night owl as a wolf that had been out on the prowl till dawn" — is an antidote to the picture of the mortally sick old man and his immense sorrow and pain.

And it is the unflinching rendition of that pain that gives *Dying Without God* its uncommon depth and beauty. In light of the great fortitude displayed by this man — continuing his opinionated lecture on life and politics, joking, generally reminiscing, railing against ex-followers who betrayed him, reflecting on personal mistakes and folly and the vanity of human wishes — who among us could measure up and soldier on as he did, resigned to his torture, handling it with such contemptuous dignity? "I suffer terribly," he says to Giesbert. "Even when I laugh." Then he adds, "But they haven't heard the last from me yet." Numberless people dwelling in the shadow of death curl up in the fetal position and blubber and pray. Not Mitterrand. Only days from the end he tells Giesbert over the phone: "Each leaf is a mirror in which the sky is reflected. My dogs are lying at my feet. In a few minutes I'm going to get up, go over to my desk, and write down what I'm thinking at this moment. Who could ask for anything more? I think I'm happy."

As *Dying Without God* closes, Mitterrand tells Giesbert, "I'd really like to be interred in the Pantheon. That's where my presidency began." I was momentarily puzzled until I quickly recalled that long-ago day in May when we writers, his spiritual brothers, stood next to him on the portico of that edifice, whose interior he had visited in an act of homage. Below the Pantheon steps, Parisians by the thousands clutched roses, socialism's emblem, and chanted, "Mitt-err-and, Mitt-err-and!" The president, smiling a thin, enigmatic smile, rocked slightly on his heels, letting the glory wash over him. There was a glow of pale and eerie light, augury of a tremendous thunderstorm approaching from the west. Below, Placido Domingo sang "La Marseillaise," and after that the Paris Opera orchestra joined with the chorus in Beethoven's "Ode to Joy." The scene was vibrant, electric, apocalyptic; for an instant the entire universe seemed to focus on the bulky, teetering figure, smiling his imperturbable smile. Thunder cracked, lightning flashed, and then the storm — as if held back by Providence until the last note of Beethoven faded away — broke in a cataclysmic torrent. The whole show seemed stage-managed, almost too glorious, as if Mitterrand had worked out a deal with Nature. "Après le déluge, moi" was of course the phrase that leaped to my mind, and I can't help but think that the president, with his fondness for aphorism, entertained the same conceit.

That was the beginning. Franz-Olivier Giesbert's stark yet tender chronicle describes the ending. The years in between will have posterity for their judge, but it is somehow good to know that after his ordeal, so nobly endured, François Mitterrand is safely past caring.

WILLIAM STYRON

Dying Without God

AUTHOR'S INTRODUCTION

*W*E SHOULD ALWAYS LISTEN to our other self, that still, small voice within that calls on us to walk in the path of righteousness, that makes us blush, bite our lips, that fills our hearts with shame whenever we are tempted to tell a lie.

François Mitterrand, who was the president of France for fourteen years, was not one to pay too much attention to that still, small voice within. He frequently said: "I don't want to be tied down. I prefer to be a free agent." Such was his basic philosophy.

As long as he was alive, Mitterrand enjoyed nothing more than breaking the rules, setting himself both above the law and above his fellow man. Let there be no mistake: this man was a Nietzschean until his dying day. That is why he always fascinated us, and why he always will. And that is also why my feelings about him are so mixed. With him, I felt a bit like Racine's Hermione:[1] I loved him too much not to hate him; I hated him too much not to love him.

There was a time many years ago when I was his pet poodle: a rather insolent poodle, to be sure, but one that would slink away to its bed at the slightest cross look from the master. Later on I became his least favorite journalist, then his bête noire—his bugbear. In his eyes, I was of no great importance. Which is as it should be. Lord knows, I've spent more years than I care to remember trying to figure out exactly who and what I am, to no avail.

He, on the contrary, had found himself. He was a Casanova of politics, always pushing himself to the limits of his ability. He knew how to turn on the charm, using his mellifluous voice to good advantage, whether in quoting the gospels when he spoke of the poor and downtrodden of the earth, whispering to the moon, or entreating the heavens to help him bring about a better tomorrow. He convinced two, perhaps even three, generations that they could transcend their limitations and rise above a world and a society in which they no longer believed. After which, the fall from grace was often hard and hurtful.

I didn't experience that rise and fall, but I don't deserve any credit. I had known Mitterrand for a long time. In fact, I was one of those starry-eyed kids from the provinces who, during the 1970s, was anxious to discover the big world and make my mark. He loved to surround himself with bright young acolytes, in order to instruct them in the finer things of life, especially literature and women. Even in those early days, his tastes and mine did not exactly coincide.

"What? You've never read Chardonne!" he would thunder.

"What? You've never read Steinbeck!" I'd shoot back.

We rarely discussed politics, but he found it hard to understand how anyone could be tempted by anything other than the exercise of power. He never for a moment doubted that his chosen profession—politics—was the best in the world, assuming one practiced it the way he did: without complexes or scruples. He loved to quote Napoleon: "First you win, then you see." He was not a Pharisee; he was the Godfather, precisely as depicted in Mario Puzo's book. He always traveled in the company of a chosen few, and nothing ever slaked his thirst, unless it was the pleasure of power.

Early during his first term in office, I had to laugh as I watched all the little lackeys trailing in his wake, polishing the floor with all their bowing and scraping, gorging themselves on his endless bounty until—imagine that!—the cupboard suddenly went bare. At which point, having been banished from the inner sanctum, they went around displaying their stigmata to one and all, crying what they thought were tears of redemption. It was all predestined. Those innocents who fattened themselves on his benevolence knew full well that Mitterrand, for all his humanity, was and remained to the end a shameless practitioner of realpolitik. If you allowed yourself to be swept up in the broad net of his considerable charm, he always assumed, as soon as he had achieved his goal, a certain smile, a smile that fooled no one. Machiavelli, Mazarin, and Richelieu, I'm sure, all had the same malevolent smile as soon as they had managed to get what they were after.

Mitterrand was both better and worse than people thought. This libertine of power loved himself too much and forgave himself everything. But he did not always lie. There were some causes he truly believed in: he did care profoundly about the wretched of the earth, those who suffered and were discriminated against. He did believe that all men are created equal—more so than he believed in the equality of the sexes, I might add. His mind was brimming with noble ideas of the century of Enlightenment, which was his spiritual home, after a slight detour at the end of the nineteenth century, to pay homage to the beginning of the Third Republic, depending on his mood. Even after the lights of the Elysée Palace had been turned off for him, at the end of his long reign, he continued to battle with all the strength at his disposal the illness that had turned his smile into a grimace and made his eyelids droop with weariness and pain, without ever losing the look of an unruly child. He was the man who always said no: no to de Gaulle, no to the Communists, no to his past, no to cancer, no to death.

When we were not angry with each other—which happened, it must be said, only a relatively few times over twenty-five years—I saw him often and listened to him carefully. He was a born orator. He spoke the way people did in the books of antiquity, his discourse laced with maxims and phrases destined to be engraved in stone. I loved it when he told me his stories, when he was relaxed and not performing on the world's stage, at which times his eyes would grow calm. What bothered me, even then, was his irony. And when he became ironic, there would be a cruel glimmer in his eyes, a bitter laugh on his lips. He had a higher opinion of himself than he did of the rest of humanity.

In short, he was an artist. His life was his work, a work that was charged and complicated, for he stemmed from and belonged to the baroque school. To give his life a unifying sense, he was forever desperately seeking a biographer, a faithful orderly who would invent his posthumous legend, which historians and chroniclers could fiddle with to their hearts' content in ages to come. For it is those—the posthumous accounts—that make men great.

But Mitterrand needed someone he could count on and talk to while he was alive, a faithful scribe who would completely efface himself behind the presidential words. He never found him. But in the solitude of the final months of his life, when most of those who had been close to him had turned their backs on him, often leaving in their wake a faint odor of rotting garbage, he occasionally called on people like me, who when he had been at the pinnacle of power had taken him to task for one thing or another, or simply been at odds with him politically. People are uncomfortable with a friend they know is dying. The specter of death makes people squirm, and so these former friends and colleagues had left him there, in his country retreat, to die alone. He did his best to fight off death's assaults, standing proud and tall, to no avail. Brought low by his illness and obsessed by posterity, he used to say to me, almost as an aside, "What I just said is for after I'm gone"; or, "You can mention that in your memoirs, if one day you should decide to write them."

I did the best I could. He would have liked to leave an indelible mark on his century, as he had left his mark on his own time. He would have liked to be de Gaulle, but unlike "the grand Charles," he had never had the chance to instill in the country he led the notion of grandeur. In the waning years of the twentieth century, Mitterrand was like everyone else: indecisive, inscrutable, and prosaic. As for my role, I am not, nor do I intend to be, what Malraux was to de Gaulle, recording the great man's message to posterity. All I have tried to do in these pages is transcribe what I saw and heard during those final weeks and months of Mitterrand's life, when the ravages of his illness were hard upon him, when death had begun to toll for him the passing bell. Born into a provincial Catholic family, he was for most of his adult life an avowed agnostic.

He was too intelligent to be an atheist, for doubt pervaded his being in matters transcendental. He did not deny the existence of God; he questioned to the very end the possibility of knowing. Thus, truly, as death moved inexorably closer, he was dying without God.

1

$\mathcal{T}$HERE ARE TIMES when you take a deep breath of fresh air that is so intoxicating it makes your nostrils quiver, your lungs tingle. There are some who say that is the definition of happiness: a sense of warmth and well-being, which often go hand in hand.

Nothing quite equals those rare moments. The breezes that slip in among people, and that waft through the trees and in among people's houses, are more than breezes: it is as if God were passing by. Often there is an aftereffect. You feel better, rejuvenated, renewed. In any case, less alone.

When I emerged from the plane that had brought me from Paris to Biarritz, I had only a few moments to savor the invigorating sea breeze of France's southwest coast before the official driver who was waiting for me at the airport whisked me away. All business, he grabbed my knapsack and tossed it into the trunk of the car. Then he literally shoved me into the back seat, climbed quickly behind the wheel, and roared away in a cloud of dust.

I was scared to death. Whenever I've been a passenger in one of those cars driven by an official government chauffeur, the same tiny fear inevitably creeps in and grabs hold of me.

I keep telling myself there's no doubt he's going to run over one of those kids darting across the street, or some old man or woman. At least a cat. Maybe a porcupine. But he never kills a thing—except my high spirits.

I don't know whether it was my state of near panic, or simply because I was growing increasingly uncomfortable as the ride went on, but each time he swerved wide left or right I began to feel sick to my stomach, so much so that I thought I was going to throw up.

"I'm not in any special hurry," I ventured.

"The president doesn't like to be kept waiting."

He was talking to me as he would have to a child. And yet he was a good twenty years my junior, and his several-day stubble, which he was obviously cultivating to make himself look older, was still little more than an adolescent fuzz.

It had been a long time since I had last visited this place. I looked around to try and spot some familiar landmarks, but found none.

"How long before we reach Latché?" I asked.

"Not long."

Doubtless to let me know he found conversation intrusive, he stepped on the gas. The car began to shake, as if it too was frightened to death.

To put up a good front and keep my hands occupied, I decided to check out the material I had brought along for the interview the president had granted me. I had packed no fewer than three tape recorders, one for my interview and two as backup, in the unlikely event that one—or even two—of the machines failed to function. A journalist's worst nightmare is one in which, despite all preparation and precautions, his tape recorder suddenly goes on the blink. I've known cases of journalists who have crossed oceans and climbed mountains to interview someone important, only to find when they got back home that all their tapes were blank.

I was changing the batteries of one of the tape recorders when the car took a sharp turn. The tape recorder fell onto the car floor and some of its innards spilled out. I groped to find the missing pieces and in so doing assumed several awkward positions, including squatting on all fours on the back seat. No luck. Another sharp turn made me lose my precarious balance and I hit my head on the car door. I cried out, less to express my suffering than to signal to the driver for God's sake to slow down! My cry fell on deaf ears. I suspected that he was secretly reveling in my obvious discomfort.

So it was that the government car finally swept into the president's residence at Latché, past the two guards standing stiffly in front of their sentry boxes.

The president was standing in the courtyard, holding a large feeding bowl in one hand. He had just finished feeding his donkeys. He gave me a quick sidelong glance, as if we had just spent the day together, and said with a half-smile, "How long has it been since you were last here at Latché? Eighteen years?"

Before I arrived he had, I was sure, checked the records to verify the date of my last visit. With death nipping at his heels, he was still leaving nothing to chance. Once again, he had figured he'd impress the hell out of me, as he had always impressed the rest of the world. It was the same old Mitterrand, the one I remembered. He knew exactly what it took to win you over. But he always went a trifle too far. One who ought to know, Ninon de Lenclos,[1] put it this way: "Nothing more agreeable than a seductive man; nothing more odious than a seducer." Most of the time, my experience had been with the seducer. For example, he figured he had won you over when, having looked you up and down the way a horse trader evaluates an animal or the way a merchant squints at a piece of fine merchandise, he addressed you as an equal, the way he would talk to some renowned expert on international affairs. Whenever he resorted to one of these tactics, I resented him for talking down to me, the way he did with so many others whom he thought he could wrap around his little finger with a well-placed compliment, a promise, or some official commendation.

There were times when he would say with great sincerity to someone, "Please do give me a call. I'd very much like to get together with you. There are all sorts of things we need to discuss." After which simpletons like me would call his office the next day, only to find that the president was all tied up and hadn't a free moment for the foreseeable future. And when next you ran into him he would blame his secretary for sheltering him from the very people he most wanted to see.

One day—Bastille Day, 1988, to be exact—during a garden party at the Elysée, the French White House, I saw the president eyeing me from across the room, then making a beeline for me through the crowd. I hadn't seen him in several years. He came straight up to me and said, "Where are you going on vacation?" I was too taken aback to say anything smart like, And what about you? Where are *you* going? Instead, I answered, "To Provence." To which he responded,

"Provence. Ah, you're still going to Provence. You're quite right to remain faithful to that lovely part of the country."

Upon which he turned on his heel and made his way back across the room.

It was the good period; it was a long time ago. I was twenty-two, he was fifty-two. I had just arrived in Paris. He had been there for a good many years. I amused him. He impressed me. He often sat down beside me and we talked: of God, of love, of books; rarely about politics. When we stuck to those general subjects, I had the feeling that I was in another, better world. Sometimes, however, he couldn't help it, his basic nature took over and he acted with me as he did with so many others. He said, as if it were the only thing in the world that mattered, "I have to make up my mind about such and such a situation. What do you think I should do?" After which, as I rambled on, flattered that I had been asked my opinion, he would depart into a kind of inner dream world, not hearing a word I was saying. Even his eyes showed he was no longer with me.

I would like to tell myself that he asked that kind of question precisely so he could escape into his own inner world. If ever you want to break off a conversation for any reason, what better way than to make the other person launch into a monologue. It's a way to leave the stage quietly, without hurting anyone. But all too aware of his methods, I knew that that attitude was a basic part of his arsenal of seduction: always make the other person feel he or she is important. Even at the risk of inflating that person's ego far more than was reasonable. Whenever you talked to him, he knew how to make you feel that you were someone he highly respected, the person who, at that moment in time, counted most in the world to him. That was the way he dealt with the fatuous and pompous, leading them down the garden path, assuming they were blind enough not to see through his little stratagems. But that was also the way he gave confidence to so many people who were shy or unsure of themselves.

"Eighteen years," he said. "That's a long time. But you'll see. Nothing has changed here. No, that is not quite true. The she-ass died, and I've replaced her. But aside from that, everything's the same. Power didn't make me rich. Look around, you can see for yourself."

He gestured broadly, the kind of gesture an innocent man makes when the police have arrived to look for proof of his guilt. "Go ahead, search the place. Empty all the drawers, you'll find nothing." But I did not respond. Even though he didn't disdain money when he had it, far from it, I knew full well that he really didn't like it, that he was sincere when he declared, at one of his party's conventions, that "money is the root of all evil." And when he denounced money, in that wonderfully convincing voice of his, I knew he meant what he said. Money *did* corrupt. In any event, maybe to prove the point, he made sure never to carry any money on him. That is doubtless why he never paid the bill when he went out to a restaurant. I take that back: when he went out with women he sometimes did. But only once in a very great while.

"I'm still living on the same modest scale," he went on, pointing to the peasant shirt he was wearing.

True. But he wasn't the type to enjoy the external trappings of wealth. If he had been a millionaire, he still would have lived as a miser. Like most of us, he preferred to amass money for his family rather than display it for all the world to see.

"You haven't changed," he said with an ironic smile.

It wasn't true of course, but I refrained from slipping into the clichéd response, "You haven't either," because it would have been patently false. Death had already inscribed itself on the face of this man who had seduced so many women. Death had also robbed him of his smile. Above all, death had already done its foul work on his eyes, from whose depths there welled a strange look, the look of the drowned, the look I remembered seeing in my mother's eyes when she finally stopped battling the cancer that was devouring her. His teeth were gray and looked as if they were on the verge of falling out. I thought back to something he had said to me many years before, as we were seated at a café in the Latin Quarter of Paris, watching the people passing by, hurrying to wherever they were heading, as city dwellers are in the habit of doing.

"One day, time has to stop," he mused, addressing himself to no one in particular. "I've always dreamed of that. A time when no one moves, when everything is frozen for all eternity. One could enjoy life better if time were to stop."

He still had not enjoyed life to the full, not enough in any case to satisfy him. The more he tried to, the more it eluded him.

"What do you say we go for a walk in the woods," he said.

Saying which, he turned on his heel and headed off. And as he suspected, I followed faithfully behind.

2

ONE DAY IN THE 1970s, as we were driving back from the provinces to Paris, Mitterrand had the driver pull over to the side of a road in the Morvan region to answer the call of nature. He preceded me into a clump of woods, where we proceeded to indulge, against the trunk of a tree, in the only human activity that relieves us of all of the world's ills. I remember him having said in a voice full of concern: "Careful, there are some primrose blooms down there."

He was the kind of man who took care where he walked, for fear of crushing the flowers, while paying little or no heed to those with him, nor to the scurrying ants or earthworms underfoot. He was utterly fascinated by everything that belonged to the plant world. Today, in the course of our walk through the woods, we were joined by Anne Lauvergeon, deputy chief of staff at Elysée, and Jacques Pilhan, the president's press advisor. Mitterrand was giving what amounted to a lecture in botany, a lecture delivered with all the authority that springs from a thorough knowledge of one's subject. Toward the end of Mitterrand's administration, Lauvergeon, a handsome woman, was the closest to him. They were always together. On this occasion, she followed the president stride for stride as she listened intently to the fruit of his erudition.

He hadn't changed. He always needed a woman in his immediate entourage, someone he could talk to. With Anne, he had chosen wisely and well. Unlike so many others, she would follow him to the very end, to his deathbed and beyond. Her eyes clearly betrayed how she felt about him: full of loyalty and compassion, yet she was nobody's fool. Her lovely eyes were those of a modern-day Florence Nightingale.

As we walked, he taught her the names of each of the plants, focusing on the genus *Dactylis*. He talked to her about the two hundred and fifty different kinds of oak trees. She was like a student in the presence of her professor, a student head over heels in love. I felt, mingling in the mellow morning air, a platonic, somewhat amused love aborning. The president never deviated from his chosen tactic for chasing skirts. His seductive voice and encyclopedic mind were his basic tools. They still worked, though now they didn't lead to anything more.

He pointed toward a nearby house. "An old peasant used to live in that house," he said. "He didn't believe in keeping his chickens cooped up, so they laid their eggs and hatched them wherever they happened to be. As a result, they began to multiply in great profusion. Chickens, you know, reproduce at a very rapid rate. Anyway, as time went on, there were chickens everywhere, under virtually every fern it seemed. Whenever you walked in this part of the woods, you would inevitably walk either on the eggs or the baby chicks. And the clucking! You can't believe the clucking that went on. Not to mention the cocks, who felt obliged to crow from dawn to dusk. No, worse: throughout the night. An impossible din."

"Why didn't nature come up with a predator to restore a semblance of order?" I asked. "A fox, some kind of predatory animal."

He smiled. I realized I had served him my question on a silver platter, enabling him to go on with his parable.

"There was a predator, but nature didn't provide it," he said. "The predator was man. One night we organized a punitive expedition to deal with the problem. We caught in our nets as many chickens as we could lay our hands on, carted them off to a place a long way from here where there was a cluster of houses, and set them loose. I assume their new neighbors knew just what to do with them."

As he smiled, one tooth, a canine if memory serves, protruded, as was often the case when he smiled. The tooth looked as if it was broken.

I didn't like his little story, the moral of which seemed to be that you shouldn't sing if you're happy. If I understood it correctly, better to cry, otherwise the gods will punish you, the way they punished the chickens and roosters of Latché. The Greeks knew that very well.

It crossed my mind that the president had doubtless too often and too openly crowed over his own happiness, to be punished the way he had been in the waning years of his second administration.

An Indian proverb teaches us: "The world flatters the elephant and flattens the ant." François Mitterrand had become an ant, dragging its feet as it moved inexorably toward its fate. We will all do the same, and in our own way.

I smiled timidly as I asked, in order to change the subject, "The end of any reign is difficult, even painful, isn't it?"

"Not only for the ruler," he said, "but for everyone involved with him as well. Remember the end of Louis XIV's reign? Far worse than mine, if you recall."

"You're right. It was pretty awful."[1]

"Or what happened at the death of Louis XV. He was so unpopular they had to build his casket in the dark of night, for fear the people might destroy it. I've not reached that point at least. What's more, think of all the heads of state who were pressured to leave office under the various Republics: Lebrun, Pétain, de Gaulle. So, I have no complaints. I'm still here, still in office."

"Still in office, true, but look what's happening. Everything is going to pot around you."

"What pains me most is the ossification of the people they've put in charge. Over the course of a few brief years, they've lost whatever imagination they might have had. If ever they did have any guts or gumption, they've lost it, so far as I can tell. They're mere shadows of their former selves. That's why any leader should always add new faces to his cabinet, replace people when the fire in their belly diminishes or dies out. I'm afraid I didn't do that often enough."

"Isn't it possible you remained in power too long? Fourteen years is a very long time for any leader, don't you agree?"

"Maybe."

"Absolutely."

He laughed, a sad little laugh, as if a sharp pain had suddenly appeared out of nowhere.

"In 1988," he went on, "I told myself that I shouldn't run for a second term. But then the temptation was just too great.

"The temptation of power."

"Yes. But I was also convinced I could win. Easily. I said to myself, I can beat those guys. Today, in my soul of souls, I tell myself the same thing."

"Do you have any regrets about having run for a second term?"

"Sometimes I feel it would have been better not to. There's something improper, something immodest, about overstaying your welcome in politics."

"In a democracy, I firmly believe it's not a good idea for one person to remain head of state for too long. But I have a strong suspicion that one of the reasons you did run for a second term was to go down in history as having been president longer than de Gaulle."

"Maybe, but I still have a long way to go to beat the real record holders, including most of the French kings, and Napoleon III. Just take a look at the Capetian dynasty: a line of fifteen kings of France. With very few exceptions—one was Louis VIII, the father of Saint Louis—they ruled between fifteen and forty-eight years. Which explains why all of them left such a firm imprint on the country."

He was just getting started: "Robert the Pious reigned from 996 to 1031; Henry I from 1031 to 1060; Philip I from 1060 to 1108; Louis VI, 'the Fat,' from 1108 to 1137; Louis VII, 'the Young,' from 1137 to 1180."

He paused, smiled, looked for something in my eyes that he didn't find, and rattled on: "Philip Augustus, reigned from 1179 to 1223. Louis VIII, 'the Lion,' from 1223 to 1226—pretty brief, that one. Saint Louis, from 1226 to 1270."

He coughed, doubtless to punctuate his effect, then: "The average declines with the son of Philip le Bel ('Philip the Handsome'). Skipping several in between, there was Charles VIII who ruled fifteen years, from 1483 to 1498; Louis XII, seventeen years, from 1498 to 1515. Francis I, thirty-two years, from 1515 to 1547."

I could see by his look that he was proud to have reeled off all these dates, which he had doubtless learned at school and presumably had revisited more recently to impress his entourage. He didn't actually reel them off: he took his time, hesitated now and then, not out of embarrassment but as if rising to the challenge. The president was doing all he could to get some sort of reaction from me, but though I was truly astonished by his unerring display of knowledge, my ignorance compelled me to silence.

"So you see," he concluded, "I'm not the first to have remained in power for a relatively long time. Nor am I the first to have a difficult end of reign."

"The future," I said, "is the past being repeated."

"Or, more precisely," he corrected, "that recycles itself. When you read de Tocqueville's *Memoirs,* you can't help but be struck by the similarity between the situations and characters he describes and those today. Read his descriptions of the revolution of 1848 and then look at today's political situation, and the people in the current parliament, and you think, Nothing has changed; the people are exactly the same as they were then. I swear it: the *very* same people. Or dip into Saint-

Simon's *Memoirs*. Same thing. He talks about people you've met or been with last evening. Only the names are different. I have the impression that 'Monsieur le Duc' or 'Harcourt' are still alive and well, right here among us."

That's the way the human race is: interchangeable and full of self-conceit. Everyone thinks he is irreplaceable, before the millstone of nature grinds him down and brings him back in another shape, for another purpose, in this story that has been described by someone as being "without a beginning, without a subject, without an end" in which all of us, big and small, powerful or powerless, live and breathe and make our daily rounds.

Take Georges Clemenceau, for example. A man for all ages. At the end of the present century he reappeared, in the guise of François Mitterrand. Both men were possessed of the same bad temper, the same love of literature, the same internal trappings. Soul mates.

When I mentioned this to Mitterrand, he shook his head in protest, saying "I wasn't nearly as spiteful as he was."

"But you're not known for being especially nice," I said.

His response, accompanied by the trace of a smile, was one I had often heard him proffer in the past: "You can't compare me with Clemenceau. I wasn't as lucky as he. I didn't have a war to deal with."

"Don't tell me that's a complaint."

"No, but I guarantee there are future historians who will denigrate me for not leading my country in wartime."

A long time earlier, François Mitterrand had confided to me that Georges Clemenceau was the personage in French history to whom he felt closest, "because of his character and the diversity of his talents." I had objected that Clemenceau had won the war but lost the peace because of the absurd Versailles treaty, which had unnecessarily humbled and humiliated Germany and subsequently turned it into a powder keg. Mitterrand had responded that it was the man who fascinated him. He also loved the fact that Clemenceau's career had blossomed so late in his life. He admired him for having become "prime minister for the first time when he was sixty-five, after having been one of the youngest members of parliament in French history."

Clemenceau, or the man who did not want to die. His life was an apologia for old age. When he was seventy-six, during World War I, he gave himself to his country and, contrary to Marshal Pétain, refused to yield to the Germans.

Mitterrand was refusing to yield to his prostate cancer. That was the war he was fighting. He kept calling in various doctors for consultations, playing one off against another as was his wont, and, like Clemenceau, mobilizing them all against the enemy that was eating away at him from within.

Clemenceau, the victor of the Great War, liked to say that he had two diametrically opposed men in his cabinet in 1917: one was a defeatist, the other a madman. Pétain and Foch. He had chosen the madman.

In fighting his cancer, Mitterrand, when all was lost, also chose the madman. He always chose the madman.

I remember having heard him say, in a paternal tone, at a time in my life when I was doing my best to turn myself into the kind of young man he wanted me to be: "Genius? What's genius? Not much really. Unrecognized geniuses are a dime a dozen. Talent? It often leads nowhere. Intelligence? Without character, it's not worth a penny. The only thing that enables you to move forward in the world is perseverance."

I totally agree. Perseverance is doubtless the only virtue worth having. After morality, to be sure.

"Persevere," he said to me. "That's the way you'll surpass the math wizards, the pencil-pushers, the bluffers, the courtesans, the facile orators, the workaholics."

Those words kept coming back to me each time I saw him, yellow as a lemon, bent over with age and pain, rowing away in his little boat into the evening of his life: "Make sure you persevere."

Like Mitterrand. Like Clemenceau.

It's probably for that reason that both men, near the ends of their lives, looked like death warmed over. Heads out of a wax museum. Both men never stopped, never looked back, and if they adopted contrarian positions whenever it suited their fancy, they never backtracked. They loathed, passionately and totally, anything that stood in their path, however trivial.

Georges Clemenceau had this to say about Aristide Briand,[2] whom he disdained: "Even when I have one foot in the grave, I'll make sure to have the other foot up that guttersnipe's rear end." Or this, about Félix Faure: "When he entered the void, he must have felt right at home." Although Mitterrand could hold his own in the witty-remarks department, he was even more pithy in describing his enemies. "That guy's a zero." "So and so? Worthless." "Who? You mean he's still alive?" He had a sharp tongue but refrained from condemnations that were overly venomous. He held back, either out of education, precaution, or perhaps superstition. He knew full well that you could never be sure which chickens might come home to roost.

That is the reason Mitterrand's blasts were far less witty than those of his spiritual predecessor, who, even on his deathbed, was still launching colorful diatribes against those he disliked or disdained.

As we emerged from the woods and began walking along the path that led up to the house, I told him this Clemenceau story that I had heard many years before, a story attributed to the French politician Édouard Herriot:[3]

> When he was on his deathbed, Clemenceau had given strict instructions that he would receive no visitors. None. Despite his order, Georges Mandel, who had been one of his closest political collaborators for many years, showed up one day to pay his respects. The governess asked him to wait in the hallway while she announced his presence. When he heard who it was, Clemenceau, in what was virtually his last breath, responded, doubtless with a derisive laugh, "Ah, yes, the worms have already begun to arrive."

Mitterrand, who had doubtless never heard the story, burst out laughing. An almost childlike laugh. Laughing at death invariably makes you younger.

Several months later, when I asked Mitterrand which person in French history he most identified with, his resemblance to Clemenceau had become total: the same hollow eyes, the same willful aggressivity, the same drawn face.

"None, really," he said. "If you're talking about the present century, I'd have to say Clemenceau, despite his enormous shortcomings. If you're talking about an earlier era, the first names that come to mind are Henry IV,[4] Mazarin,[5] Condorcet,[6] Vauban . . .[7]

"Why Vauban?"

"He was a man of relatively modest origins or, to be fairer, from the minor aristocracy. In the seventeenth century, on the strength of his merits alone, he rose to become a French marshal. We all know what a military genius he was, and all the work he did in fortifying the cities of France. But he was also a free spirit who wanted freedom and justice for all French citizens. But when in 1707, near the end of his life, he published, without authorization from the king, his *Project for a Royal Tithe,* he fell into disfavor and was exiled to his country estate near Vézelay, a region near and dear to me. In my opinion, Vauban was the living incarnation of the well-balanced Frenchman.

"And if you go even further back in time?"

"How far back? To Vercingetorix?"[8]

"You mean you like losers?"

The death mask managed a smile, a sardonic smile, although I knew it was meant to be friendly.

"Since we're on the subject of Vercingetorix," Mitterrand went on, "qualifying him as a loser is simply wrong. True, the Gauls of the time were not capable of resisting the well-oiled Roman military machine, but the fact is, Vercingetorix did hold off the Romans for a long time. And don't forget, it was at the Gallic oppidum of Bibracte that the first attempt was made to unify France. Is it fair to speak of

'French unity' way back then? Probably not, but it was there that the Gallic chieftains swore allegiance to a single leader, namely Vercingetorix. For the first time the Gallic tribes, whole provinces in fact, represented by their local leaders, felt their fortunes were bound up with one another."

"Are you implying that the embryo of the French nation appeared that day?"

"France didn't exist, of course, so the answer has to be no. But you can say that it was an initial attempt at unifying the Gauls."

"When would you say that France actually came into being?"

"That's a subject of considerable debate. Often heated debate, I might add. If you want my immediate reaction, I'd say Philip Augustus.[9] First and foremost, he was a winner. He played an important role in Europe. And he was also a legislator. By building the Louvre tower, he gave France a true symbolic center. Having said all that, I have to add that there was a great deal that had to be done after Philip Augustus before France became truly unified. So I have to qualify that choice, which is a bit arbitrary. On second thought, one could argue that France was really born with Charles V."[10]

He bit his lip, but I noted there wasn't much lip left to bite.

He was wound up now, and went on at full speed. "I forgot," he said, shaking his head, "the king who was doubtless the greatest figure of all French history, Charles VII. It's strange to think how few biographies of him there are. A victim of posterity. And yet it was he who unified France in the fifteenth century. He gave it a real set of laws, put it on a sound financial basis, gave the country confidence in itself. When he came to power in 1422, almost all of France was occupied by the English, and thirty years later they had virtually been chased from the country, hanging onto only the port of Calais. But despite all his successes, he had the misfortune to have been overshadowed by Joan of Arc. She pushed him into the shadows. During his lifetime, I'm sure he figured that this slip of a lass from Domremy was of little or no importance, that she'd be ignored or forgotten by history. But in fact, from his reign, she's the only figure people do remember."

Who was president of France during the times of Jean Jaurès, Claude Monet, Marcel Proust, or Jacques Prevert? Who was king during the times of Rembrandt, van Gogh, or Spinoza? François Mitterrand had a hard time accepting the fact that history is kinder to artists, writers, and philosophers than it is to politicians. Despite all his protestations to the contrary, and his declarations proclaiming himself a friend of the arts, his real affinities were with those in positions of power.

Often, death deals with such people with disrespect, or even disdain.

When I asked him who was his least favorite person in French history, he replied without hesitation, "Talleyrand."[11]

"On the human level or politically?"

"I loathe him because he sold France down the river."

"Because he betrayed Napoleon?"

"No. Because, as I just said, he *sold* France. To any and all bidders."

"Did you think highly of Napoleon?"

"He was a very great man, but if you were to draw up a list of all his pluses and minuses, the balance sheet would have to be negative as far as France is concerned."

"One could even make a case for those who maintain that he shrank the country. One historical study shows that during his reign the average height of the French recruits decreased by almost an inch."

"Are you sure that the average height of French soldiers actually *increased* during the years I was in power?"

And he began to rub his hands together. Big hands. Strange hands. Had they been fashioned specifically to caress women? Or to strangle men?

3

$\mathcal{B}$ACK FROM OUR WALK, we sat down on some lounge chairs set beneath the branches of a tall tree whose protection had something maternal about it. We were comfortable there, completely at ease. I made the mistake of bringing the conversation back to Clemenceau.

"His major mistake," I said, "was loving money too much."

By the twitch just above his left eye, I could tell the remark irritated Mitterrand.

"What do you mean by that?" he asked.

"That despite his many qualities, somewhere the man was corrupt."

"Ah?"

The president had a startled look, the way a lady of the high aristocracy might look if she discovered the droppings of a fox in her rose garden. I was pleased that my remark had had its effect, but I felt I should clarify my assertion. "Clemenceau was a great man, no question. The problem is, he wasn't clean."

Mitterrand shrugged. "Not clean, not clean. How you do go on. Because you believe that people get involved in politics in order to line their pockets?"

"No. But I don't think I'm exaggerating when I say that one doesn't preclude the other. Take Talleyrand, for instance."

The president sighed noisily, to show his increasing irritation.

"What primarily interests a politician," he said, rubbing his hands together again, "is not money. It's power. That's all he thinks about, day and night. If he spends his weekends shaking hands, listening to the idle prattle of his constituents, or driving hundreds of miles in a day, it's because of power. If he sacrifices everything—his family, his health, his dignity—it's always because of power. He conducts his life in order to become some high-ranking government official, or president. *Not* to fatten his bank account."

I thought back to the François Mitterrand I had known in the 1970s, to the days we had spent together. He was a monk-soldier, a Spartan, an insomniac, a man who had the ability to use his body to the maximum. He didn't haul it along. It hauled him.

One day I remarked to him that he had apparently absorbed and applied the lesson of the Buddha: "Man is born alone, lives alone, and dies alone; and it is man alone who carves out the path along which he walks."

"And that's why I've always gone on carving away," he responded.

He was like those who don't know when or how to stop. Neanderthal man had reappeared in him. He often forgot to shave and never smelled like a rose. Looking at his shoes, you might well conclude that they had weathered at least one war. They had never seen a shoeshine brush, of that you could be sure.

But he did brush his teeth, I can attest to that. One morning, when we were in Chatellerâult, he had loaned me his tube of toothpaste. And years later, when he was talking about me to mutual friends—when we were on the outs—he said, only half jokingly, "What a terrible man Giesbert has turned into. When I think of all the things we shared together!"

In those earlier days, I had often followed him during his electoral campaigns, as a correspondent for the Paris weekly magazine *Nouvel Observateur*. At the hotel, we often had adjoining rooms. And when he had to be up at the crack of dawn, it was he who would wake me up with a knock on my door. We talked endlessly. He taught me about life, about women, told me where the best places in the country were to stay and have a good meal.

He also taught me how to travel light when I was covering his campaigns into the further reaches of France. "No suitcase," he instructed. "All you need is your razor, your toothbrush, a tube of toothpaste, a change of shirt, a change of socks, all of which you can fit in your briefcase. Plus a book, of course. Always remember to take along a book."

Up at six and in bed the next morning at two, the young François Mitterrand was off to spread the good word about socialism in the back rooms of the grassroots faithful. No matter how insipid the comments of his constituents, how long-winded and pointless their stories, he always listened as if he cared, really cared, about their petty local disputes, their children's studies, their latest gastronomic delectations. He seemed deeply interested in everything they said. He knew how to pretend.

That has to be the most wearying thing in life: pretending. I would never have been able to hide my irritation in the presence of stupidity. I would have been too afraid that such repression would have made my cells explode.

From a tree somewhere in the garden came the cries of birds that had been suddenly disturbed. Perhaps by a cat passing by, or a hawk. The president paid not the slightest heed. Had it been the murmur of pine needles in the wind, he would have looked up.

"If politicians are obsessed only with the idea of winning, of holding onto power," I began, "why are so many of them corrupt?"

"Because money is often available for the asking."

"There are also cases where they do everything in their power to seek it out."

"In that case, it's because some politicians think they're above the law. It's a classic phenomenon: when you've reached the top of the mountain you don't look down. You think you've 'arrived.' Take any of the political scandals you can think of. What's most amazing about all of them is how easy it was to catch the guilty party. You wonder how they could have been so stupid."

"They simply weren't able to resist temptation."

The president shook his head, smiled a knowing smile, and said, "You're not telling me anything I don't already know.

History abounds with people who haven't been able to resist temptation. The current wisdom is that corruption is a new phenomenon. Not so. I could name you a dozen famous political figures from the past without even trying, from Richelieu to Mirabeau. And what about Danton, who stole the justice department blind? And Talleyrand, who after he had been named minister of foreign relations under the Directory, exulted: "And now I must amass a fortune. An immense fortune"?

He took a deep breath. The sea breeze was coming in off the Atlantic, and he wanted to fill his lungs with it.

I wondered if he hadn't used the past to prove that everything was relative, and thus in a way absolve himself and his administration of the petty scandals that had beset them over the past several years.

A rogue is a rogue is a rogue, no matter what period you're referring to. Sometimes these gentlemen make a point of preaching, of being holier-than-thou. Sometimes they end up in prison. Sometimes in sumptuous palaces. And some are accorded national funerals, with all the pomp and circumstance they don't deserve.

I don't know why, but I always think of the president and one of his favorite rogues each time I remember Chateaubriand's words on the subject of corruption: "Suddenly a door opens: vice enters silently, clinging to the arm of crime, Monsieur Talleyrand held up by Monsieur Fouché."

I don't know why, because François Mitterrand is neither vice nor crime. He was no more than an Epicurean, who had raised pleasure, and above all the pleasure of ruling, into a virtue. He couldn't help it. That was the principal sin of which he was accused, although it was only one among several.

"When I leave office," he said, "I won't be a penny richer than I was when I was sworn in almost fourteen years ago. That can be proved, since when I leave office I plan to make public a full breakdown of my net assets." A smile. "Of course, what *won't* be made public are my countless Swiss bank accounts." A laugh. "They'll be very difficult to keep track of." Another laugh. "There are so many I can't keep track of them myself." A loud guffaw. "I can't even remember the banks' addresses any more."

A moment of self-satisfied silence.

"Did you hear the latest rumor about my vast wealth?" he said. "Apparently, so the story goes, I have a palace in Venice."

Suddenly he grew serious again. A flash of pain or despondency appeared on his furrowed brow.

"You know very well how little money means to me," he went on.

All you had to do was look at the man, poorly dressed in his ragged old shirt and baggy trousers, which doubtless had been manufactured from some inexpensive fabric.

I was tempted to reply that, while I knew for a fact he wasn't interested in money per se, he did like people for whom money was the focus and goal of their existence. I had a feeling he had read my thoughts.

"And what about Pelat, you'll say?"

Pelat was an old friend of Mitterrand's, a sometime businessman who had run afoul of the law. I could have mentioned other names as well. The profiteers and traffickers circle around power the way moths do around lights at night, and François Mitterrand had the gift of taking them under his wing. But Pelat was a very special type. He had made his way in the world by sheer force of will and hard work, the capacity for both of which he had in spades. He had been an apprentice butcher, a waiter in a café, and an assembly line worker in the Renault automobile factory before the war. He had met François Mitterrand in a prisoner-of-war camp in 1940, not far from Weimar: Stalag 9A in Thuringia. After which he had been in the French underground, then after the war had gone into business. And, in whatever role or position he found himself, he was also one of the world's great practical jokers. In fact, he was a very funny man, this two-sided swashbuckler, even when he wasn't trying. Many's the time I've seen Pelat and Mitterrand laughing their heads off at some mutually shared story or joke.

"He was my friend," Mitterrand said simply. "I really liked him. He fascinated me, I must confess. He was a true original, a force of nature. When he was back on his farm, he used to drive the tractor himself. And he was one of the funniest men who ever lived. But, it's also true he was someone who refused to live by the rules of society. A rebel. If someone gave him a hot tip and there was money to be made, he didn't hesitate for a moment. I always knew that. That's why, despite all my affection for him, I never agreed to have dinner at his house. Not once. Check that out if you want."

Better not check that out, I decided, since I was sure he was lying.

Money has no odor, but its servants all smell. Often of petticoats. Sometimes of mink. Sometimes of horses. I've often wondered how the president of France could accept to live in the midst of this menagerie where everyone had their fingers in the pie. In the long run, he couldn't help hating himself.

But I think he loved himself too much for that.

Legends arrive without your seeing them coming. They slip in from behind, on the sly. By virtue of repetition, they transform themseves into revealed truths.

Thus it was that François Mitterrand became, in the eyes of so many of his peers, one of the great villains of French history, "Uncle Money-Grubber." And yet he wasn't a man to whom money meant very much. He could never even add up a column of figures properly. Zeros were more than he could manage. What he prized above all was monkish sobriety, which he imposed wherever he went, and that included the tiny room with whitewashed walls, on the avenue Frederic-Le Play, where he breathed his last.

I've already mentioned that he never paid. Whenever he went out to a restaurant, or anywhere else for that matter, he faithfully managed to avoid picking up the check. But, on the contrary, he was terrible at making others pay what they owed him. "During the '60s and '70s, when I was practicing law," he once told me, "I had a problem: my clients took advantage of me, almost without exception. First there was a man named Rinaldi, a Corsican who was trafficking in counterfeit paintings, who told me the first time I ever met him, 'When I arrived here on the mainland for the first time I did exactly what the Pope always does, I knelt down and kissed the earth.' He had made a vow that he would never do a day's work in his life, no matter what. His vow was fulfilled. And, I might add, he never paid me a penny for my legal services. But he was an extremely likable man. Then there was this Italian millionaire whose case I defended. When the trial was over he came over to me and said, 'Sorry, I can't pay you. I'm wiped out. Ruined. Would you mind lending me a little money, just enough so I can get a bite to eat?' I gave him two hundred francs—the equivalent of about forty or fifty dollars in those days. It was lunch hour. I had a date for lunch with someone, and my Italian asked if he could come along. When we left the courtyard, there waiting for him at curbside was his liveried chauffeur, holding the car door open for us. The car? A Bentley, no less.

"And then there was this Canadian client who once invited me to the restaurant in the poshest hotel in Monaco. When it came time for the check, he suddenly began patting his suitcoat pocket, and said: 'Damn, how stupid of me! I forgot my wallet.' And to show how stupid *I* was, I kept him as a client."

True, Mitterrand was not money-minded, but he had also understood that money was the best friend of power, to which he sacrificed everything—his life, his work, his morality.

Money protects, purifies, and exalts. That in any event is what the realists—those of little imagination—believe. François Mitterrand was a realist, as I've already said. He had far too much to do to care about money, whether in the getting or the spending. But he needed it. For women, for his children, for later.

He never solicited or sought money for himself. But he

did nothing to stop those among his friends and colleagues, who robbed the country blind without a pang of conscience. And holding high the banner of socialism as they robbed. He let them do their evil deeds, but at the same time he despised them for it, for he could never manage to still completely the voice of the other Mitterrand, the voice that had his mother's country accent. It said to him, Money is the blood of the poor. For centuries people have lived from it and died from it. It encapsulates and encompasses all human suffering.

He despised them, but he endured them, even encouraged them. Not because he received anything in return, but rather because his motto was: "once a friend always a friend." He was faithful only to his friends. He allowed the most dubious, the least acceptable, to remain at his side, even unto death. Beyond death. He refused to judge them. "People are not either white or black," he used to say. "They're all varying shades of gray."

In this instance, François Mitterrand was also gray, like all the cats at night.

4

$\mathcal{W}$E WERE TAKING A STROLL through his country property. The pine needles formed a kind of cushion underfoot, and it was soft to walk on, as if we were walking on butter. The president seemed to glide, as he had always glided through life.

I had never understood how this earthling, with his big feet, had always managed to walk so lightly. No matter how solemn or official the occasion, he always seemed to be walking on air. Unlike most heads of state, whose steps were like forceful hammer blows, his never were. He always gave the impression that he was arriving on little cat feet, as if by surprise.

We were talking about René Bousquet, who had served as secretary general of the police in the collaborationist Vichy government during World War II. Mitterrand had gone on seeing him for many years after the war, in fact up until the time when Bousquet had been officially accused of crimes against humanity for his role in the roundup of Parisian Jews at the Vélodrome d'Hiver—Paris's Madison Square Garden—in the winter of 1942. Over a two-day period, January 16 and 17, 12,884 Jews, foreigners, and stateless men, women, and children were arrested and sent to the death camps. René Bousquet was the organizer of the roundup. I told Mitterrand how surprised I was that he had gone on seeing this former associate of Marshal Pétain, which struck me at best as an indulgence and at worst an act of culpability.

"I didn't see that much of him," he said. "And starting in 1986 I severed all relations. This said, I really did like the man. He had an incredible gift of gab."

"Didn't you have the feeling you were compromising yourself by seeing him?"

"No. He had been cleared of all crimes by the tribunals of the liberation, which as you know were extremely tough. All the honors and decorations that had been bestowed on him were restored. He had collaborated, no question about it, but he had also aided the French resistance."

"But why did you go on seeing him after he had been implicated in the roundup of Jews at the Vél d'Hiv?"

"I believe in the presumption of innocence about people, until I'm proven wrong. And besides, I never turn my back on my friends."

"But Bousquet wasn't a friend."

"True. But he was a close acquaintance."

"What was so special about him?"

I remember that just then there was a moment of silence, as a little gust of wind passed between us. The president paused and stared at me for several seconds, before his lips formed a tiny smile. "It was my bad side," he said, then his smile broadened, revealing his gray teeth. "Riff-raff," he said. "I've always had a weakness for rogues and scoundrels."

He had spoken about them, the down and dirty, the

way he would have referred to a dish on the menu, with delectation.

"He was the kind of person I've always found amusing," he murmured, "an adventurer."

I knew very well what he liked in other people. He really enjoyed, and got along with, only those who took full responsibility for their own actions, people who had the courage to break with society's taboos—taboos that he himself was incapable of breaking. He liked people who were playful, bawdy, libertine. That was why, no matter where he was or under what circumstances, there was always an aura about him of off-color laughter, of dirty jokes being told.

If at times he assumed a royal bearing, that of Louis XIV in the presence of his court—lips pursed, gaze heavenward, very high and very far away—he never mistook himself for a king. But like royalty he needed fools or buffoons around him. Over the last few years, that, it seemed, was all he had in his entourage: so many political nonentities, all of whom came bearing their parcels of farces and practical jokes. They all knew how to get his attention.

"You know the latest joke making the rounds, Mr. President?" And already the presidential nostrils would begin to quiver, the lips to purse in anticipation of the laughter to follow.

A king without diversion is an unhappy king.

He cured his bouts of acute anxiety by making endless phone calls, by hopping into the presidential helicopter for a quick trip to somewhere or nowhere, or by indulging in merrymaking of one sort or another. He always had to be thinking of something else or keeping his mind occupied. That was why he had such an insatiable need for power.

A long time ago, when we were taking a train trip together, he leaned over and asked, with that penetrating tone he always adopted when he was making fun of the world: "Power. What does that mean to you?"

I wasn't quite sure just how to answer such a question, but I smelled a rat. After a moment's reflection, I decided to quote Henry Kissinger, whose memoirs I had just finished reading: "An aphrodisiac," I said, half jokingly.

"It's true that I don't know a single head of state who hasn't yielded to some kind of carnal temptation, small or large. That in itself is reason enough to govern. I remember Le Troquer, who at the time was president of the National Assembly and whose body was visibly in serious decline. Each time he ran into me he would point to his crotch and say, with the smile of a conqueror, 'Everything else may be falling apart, but that is still in good working order!' "

I reminded him of one of Napoleon's well-known private jokes, which was his habit of calling out to Josephine, "Don't bother washing! I'll be right there!"

"Are you sure that wasn't Henry IV?" Mitterrand responded. Then, with a knowing smile: "And what about de Gaulle?"

"True. He seems to be the exception that proves the rule. No straying from the straight and narrow, so far as I know. But de Gaulle wasn't a man; he was an idea. He was France incarnate, and France couldn't be laid."

A shrug of the presidential shoulders.

"De Gaulle was enamored of power," he protested.

"That's all he did love. But he was neither Snow White nor Joan of Arc. Even if, late in life, there are no stories I'm aware of that he was ever involved with any women."

To lighten the atmosphere, I turned back to the question we had been discussing earlier, and mentioned one definition of power that Edgar Faure, the former prime minister, had given me one day: "Power," he had said, "is water. It's forever slipping through your fingers."

"He knew what he was talking about. Power was forever slipping between his fingers."

"But who ever does manage to hold onto it?"

"Good question. The answer is, no one."

"Faure also added this: 'Power is water, which enables you to wash your hands of everything else.' "

"I'd say rather that power is a pot too full: water keeps spilling over its sides. Power is a quest, an obsession. Something that takes hold of you when you're young and never lets go, and yet it's something no one ever succeeds in keeping."

That goes a long way toward explaining why one had the sense that François Mitterrand was always dissatisfied. I can still recall the plaintive tone in his voice, back in 1982, when he had at his disposal the rather extraordinary prerogatives bestowed on him by the constitution of the Fifth Republic. "The conservatives control the financial world and the vast majority of the administrative positions in the country. They control the banks, big business, the press. What do I control? Nothing!"

"You have the executive *and* the legislative powers. What more could you ask for?"

"What you don't understand," he retorted, "is that I have

no control over the inner workings of the country. I spend my time pushing all kinds of buttons that simply don't respond. The conservatives have their people in positions of power, and although we liberals won the elections, those same people are still in place."

"But you fired a goodly number of them."

"Clearly not enough. Our problem is, we're much too nice. Which explains why I have no real power."

The more he coveted power, the less he felt he had. Within a few months of his inauguration he dominated France politically, and yet France seemed to be like quicksand beneath him.

I'm not sure that really bothered him all that much. Although he was not a man to be satisfied with appearances, he was far too lucid to imagine that he could ever dominate the elements. He knew all too well that one day, sooner or later, the elements would dominate him and that his condition would not protect him since, to paraphrase Aeschylus, Zeus's bolts of lightning generally strike the mountain peaks.

I know the image will seem grandiloquent, but as we were walking though the pine woods the president paused, looked as if he were filling his soul with fresh air, and thrust out his chest. He was hatching something and it wasn't an egg.

"Do you know the story about the incoming president?"

The way he looked at me I could tell it was a rhetorical question. There was a twinkle in his eye. He went on. "At the inauguration of the new president, the outgoing president handed his successor three numbered envelopes. 'Each time you run into a major crisis,' he said, 'open one of these numbered envelopes. It will enable you to deal with the crisis.' Three months after the new president had taken the oath of office, the country was completely paralyzed by a major strike. The chief of state decided it was time to open the first envelope, which said: 'Blame the problem on your predecessor.' So he went on nationwide television and proclaimed: 'It's all the fault of our former president.' And the strike quickly ended. A year later, there was another major strike. He opened the second letter, which read: 'Blame everything on a combination of circumstances resulting from the unfortunate international situation.' So he followed the advice in the envelope, with the same positive results. Two years later, the country was hit by another major crisis: the postal system was in disarray, as was the entire transportation sector; the gas and electricity workers were out on strike. Chaos everywhere you looked. In every city throughout the country people were marching in the streets. So the president decided it was high time to open the third envelope, which said: 'Prepare three envelopes.' "

He waited until I had stopped laughing, planted his cane solidly in the pine needles, leaned heavily against it, and breathed in deeply several times, as if each might be the last.

"I love the sea air," he said. "Because of the salt."

I think he was trying to tell me something, but I wasn't quite sure what, and I decided not to press the issue but bring the conversation back to what we had been talking about earlier: political power.

"So if power doesn't exist," I said, "then what is politics after all?"

"What is politics?" he repeated, his eyes squinting as if he were looking for an answer. But he had already found it.

"Our esteemed former prime minister, Aristide Briand, gave what I think is the best definition: 'Politics,' he said, 'consists of saying things to people.' "

I didn't buy that vague definition. For one thing, it stank of a "what's-the-use" attitude, for it justified all the charismatic rulers, all the eloquent orators of history who either lulled their people into a state of passivity or sent them off to be killed in one war or another. If these rulers had a burning desire to win at all costs, which remains to be proved, then nothing is worth anything and, therefore, anything goes. I've always preferred Jefferson to Washington, Condorcet to Robespierre, Bismarck to Kaiser Wilhelm II. I said so to the president, reminding him of the words of another prime minister, Edouard Daladier, the man who had signed the Munich accord in 1938, that famous agreement which, in the words of his fellow signee Neville Chamberlain, would bring "peace in our time." Politics, Daladier once noted, is neither logical nor rational. For the most part, it's an irrational dynamic.

Mitterrand looked at me strangely and murmured: "Why 'for the most part?' It's *always* irrational."

I was certain he really didn't believe that. He looked away with a weary expression that clearly indicated he would prefer to change the subject.

5

$\mathcal{T}$HE PRESIDENT LEFT ME TO MY OWN DEVICES, having business to take care of with Jacques Pilhan. Officially, Pilhan was one of Mitterrand's media advisors. But he was also a political strategist known for his fondness for blitzkrieg techniques. Pilhan's nickname was Knight of the Decline because of his steadfast loyalty to Mitterrand to the bitter end. He had been following discreetly in our footsteps during our walk. An aggressive, arrogant man, he tended to become belligerent when times were tough. He was the last ace of clubs in the final hand of Mitterrand's card game.

"If I were to become senile," Mitterrand was asking him, "would you tell me so?"

Pilhan shrugged, with a certain insolence I thought, as if astounded by the stupidity of the question. He was prince of the Pygmalions. He could do or say anything he pleased.

"Of course I would, Mr. President."

"I'm counting on you."

"You may."

"But I'm sure you won't keep your word."

Anne Lauvergeon broke into the conversation, with the authority of a registered nurse, an affectionate authority.

"There's no question of your becoming senile," she protested. "You shouldn't even talk that way, Mr. President."

A few days earlier, after she had remonstrated with him in a similar way, he had said, "Come now, the moment I die all you'll be thinking about is what dress you'll be wearing to my funeral. Don't fret too much about it in any case; there won't be many people there." At which point he smiled at her mischievously, then apologized, "I'll have to ponder that a bit, you know. The vise is tightening. I can feel it in my bones."

He who enjoyed looking at things from an angle looked death straight on. For a long time he had been under the impression that fate would deal him a death not unlike that of Charles Quint who, three weeks before rendering his soul, participated in his own requiem mass. Later on, Mitterrand concluded that illness would condemn him to a lingering end, like that of Louis XIV as described by the historian Saint-Simon, when each succeeding day is one more step downward toward the next world, which you end up facing alone and on your knees.

"I'm not at all sure I'll be able to hang on till the end of my second term," Mitterrand said. "If I do, it'll be a real accomplishment."

A yellow smile, that of a lemon that had fallen from the tree and lain on the ground for some time.

"A pity, but I have a feeling I'll miss it by about two months. Just think. Two lousy months!"

He looked really upset and unhappy.

I had often talked to him about death. He approached it with detachment, as if it were a raging toothache, no more, and yet he gave the impression that that was all he thought of, for the question kept cropping up time and again in every conversation. And besides, for some time now he had been an obsessive visitor to cemeteries.

One day I had said to him, "It's strange, but dead friends are often closer to me than the living. They live in us."

"Have you noticed that, too?"

"The older you are, the more dead souls you have in your head. At your age, there must be a real crowd."

"Absolutely. I'm in the same situation in that regard as anyone past seventy. The dead are accumulating around me, and I'm beginning to feel a bit lonely."

"Not all that lonely, since you have them living with you in your mind. Do you ever talk with them?"

"No. That is, with only a few. It's possible I talk to friends I was especially close to, people who died without properly saying good-bye. I tell them how I feel about them. But I wouldn't pride myself on it. In general, I think it's safe to say I'm not a great communicator. Even during periods when I withdraw within myself, what religious people call meditating. At night, before I go to bed and start to read, I think of all the people I've loved during my life. In fact, not a day goes by when I don't think of them."

"Who do you think of most often?"

A melancholy sigh, like the hissing of air leaving a balloon. "First and foremost, my parents. Then friends who were near and dear to me who died a long time ago: Georges Dayan[1] and his brother Jean. And Jean Riboud.[2] I think of him a great deal because I was so impressed with the way he dealt so courageously with his lung cancer, up to the very end. And Jean Chevrier, owner of the Vieux Morvan Hotel, whom

I saw every week at Château-Chinon[3] and who managed to harbor an enormous amount of subtlety and good taste beneath a veneer of good old common sense. And then there's a Jesuit priest you've never met, a slightly marginal cleric who nonetheless had a considerable influence on me."

With which he strode off purposefully, as if he were in a great hurry. "I'm not afraid of death, you know. It's been my companion for too long now for me to be afraid."

"When you reach a certain age you end up accepting it. It becomes a chore you simply can't avoid."

"We tell ourselves that it awakens us from the dream that life was."

He talked to me about the poet Max Jacob, who was arrested during World War II by the Germans. He spent four days after his arrest at the Orleans Prison, before being shipped to a concentration camp and death. During those four days, he danced and sang Offenbach songs to the other prisoners. What Mitterrand liked, and found most remarkable, was that false frivolity, that real insolence in the face of destiny.

"But it's your perfect right not to like or agree with that posture," he went on. "Casanova made a number of very pertinent observations about death." He squinted, as if digging in his memory, and came up with the following—a quote I have since verified: "Death is a monster that chases from the great theater an attentive spectator, before a play that interests him greatly is over. That reason alone is sufficient for one to loathe death."

"There's only one thing that really bothers me," he went on. "Suffering. It's as though I have a knife stuck in me, a knife that's taking my life drop by drop. I'd have so much preferred to die swiftly. Boom, gone!"

"The other side of that coin is that you wouldn't have had time to prepare yourself," I protested. "Seneca has taught us that it's good to see death coming, so you can tame it."

"I would have preferred to go like Jean Dayan, who died in his sleep. When they found him, there wasn't the slightest expression of pain or anguish on his face. Nothing. He was lying on his side, completely at peace. Normal. There were a number of cigarette butts in the ashtray by his bed."

He paused beside an herb, cut it with his fingernails, caressed it with his fingertips, then closed his eyes as if overcome by a sort of inner happiness. "The worst thing," he said, "is that all around me people are dropping like flies. Before long it'll be a real wasteland. If it goes on this way, I soon won't have anyone with whom I can share old memories. Perhaps that's the hardest part of growing old. As for the rest . . ."

"The rest. What do you think of as 'the rest?' "

"Not very much. Rheumatism. Aches and pains."

He laughed, that is he tried to laugh, but it wouldn't come. Not enough air in his lungs.

"I suffer terribly, as you can see," he said. "Even when I laugh. At night, whenever I wake up I feel afraid. Not at the thought of death, but because I realize I'm going to have to face another day of excruciating pain."

Again he laughed, an icy laugh that chilled me to the bone; the same hissing sound of air escaping from a balloon.

"But they haven't heard the last of me yet. My family has a history of longevity. I have several aunts who lived to be a hundred. A number of uncles who lived to be over ninety.

Meanwhile, the most embarrassing part of this situation is that everyone tends to bury you alive. No one even makes an effort to come and see me any longer. I've even had to cancel the private screenings at the Elysée Palace. People kept calling to beg off. 'Please tell the president we're terribly sorry but we won't be able to make it tonight.' No matter, I wasn't enjoying those evenings anymore anyway. I have the feeling I'm in the process of tiptoeing away from everything."

"I have a friend who used to say: 'There are people whom life leaves and there are those who leave life.' "

"It often comes to the same thing. If you leave life, it's generally because life is in the process of abandoning you, and because those things you've always done automatically, by reflex—breathing, chewing, moving your arms—have now become painful. One of my friends whose wife had recently died of cancer decided he would die, too. Somehow he managed to come down with cancer, and a few months later he joined his wife. But he didn't die of cancer. He died of a broken heart."

He called out to his Labrador, Baltique, who had wandered off into the ferns. The dog came running back so promptly that the president, proud of having made such a show of authority, couldn't help smiling with satisfaction.

"If only they all were like Baltique," he sighed. "You have no idea of the extent of the betrayals, my ex-colleagues who have disappeared into the night."

"When the oak falls, everyone becomes a woodcutter."

"In my case, the woodcutters are in such a hurry they've started to cut me up even before the tree has fallen."

He looked pained, as if recalling all the people who had betrayed his trust, but I felt the expression was insincere.

"Among the woodcutters, I found all sorts of people I would never have expected. People who professed to be my most loyal and faithful friends. Real zealots. I must say I was truly surprised. I've often been accused of being too cynical when it comes to my fellow man. It's been said that I use them, play on their shortcomings and failings. But when you see what's going on today, you have to admit I was right, no?"

His voice was angry, but it was an anger stripped of all strength, a quavering voice.

"All my former faithful followers lining up to jump on me. Most of them owe me everything politically, and yet here they are in essence spitting at me in the face. Really disgusting. Obviously, it's easy enough to do now."

"Louis XIV used to say that as soon as a king wavers about a decision he has made or an order he has given, all authority vanishes, and peace of mind as well."

"He was right. But all that proves is that there's nothing new under the sun. Death brings us back to our rightful place, that is to say, nowhere."

He said that with an air that was both weary and regal.

"It's been said of you that you reek of heresy," I ventured.

"I'm sure that's also been said of everyone who's played a major role in public life. Just go back and look at all the negative things they said about Clemenceau. But it's true that I've had my fair share, too."

I commented that he had frequently provoked the polemics by constantly reinventing the novel of his own life. After having spent so much time and effort trying to make us believe the moon was made of green cheese, I said, he should not be surprised, as more and more about him was revealed over the years, that we came to believe it wasn't.

Lies don't grow old. They rot immediately, and it is out of their dunghill that slander is born.

"Why did you hide for such a long time the fact that you met Pétain?" I asked.

He acted as if he wanted to make sure he understood my question. "Why?" His eyes circled the distant horizon, then he launched into a detailed explanation.

"Take a look at the chronology. After having been captured by the Germans and interned as a prisoner of war, I escaped from the prison camp near the end of 1941. I didn't get involved in anything until February or March 1942. In June of that year, I took part in an organized meeting held by former prisoners of war who had escaped. A meeting to organize a resistance movement. More or less at the same time, various POW centers—of which I was one of the leaders—joined forces to try and raise money to send our comrades still held in prison camps. Pétain asked us to come and see him. I and three other directors of the movement did go and see Pétain, one of whom was my good friend Marcel Barrois—who was the head of our group. He by the way was subsequently arrested, deported, and died in a concentration camp. My so-called relations with Pétain were limited to that one brief meeting. After that I took part in various resistance movements, and by the time I was twenty-five I was one of the leaders. In March 1944, General de Gaulle named me as one of the fifteen men who, under the direction of Alexandre Parodi, would head up the state during the early transition days following the liberation. On August 19, 1944, I took over as the Commissioner General of Prisoners of War. In his *Memoirs,* General de Gaulle cited me as one of those who, at great personal risk, was responsible for the liaison between England and France, both by plane and by boat, in the dark of night."

"If you were attacked for what you did during the war, it was also because of the award you were given by Marshal Pétain."

"That so-called award was given to the principal directors of *all* social organizations. It also served as an excellent cover. And, if you want to carry the point to its absurd conclusion, I might point out that the first time I escaped from a German prison camp I walked for twenty-two days and twenty-two nights, from Thuringia to the Swiss border, in the bitter cold, often in the snow. And during the entire time I was wearing a little insignia on my raincoat, a Nazi insignia. I can't tell you how pleased I was the day I happened to find it. Foolishly pleased, I might add. Now don't tell me that because I wore that Nazi pin on my lapel for three weeks I'll be accused of being a Nazi."

He laughed; he had made his point. When I asked him whether he had ever flirted with the far right, he who was known to have revered Colonel de Rocque, an ultra-extremist, and actually worked as a young volunteer for his cause, fluttered his eyes and responded, with no noticeable elongation of his nose, "I *never* flirted with the far right. I was always a firm believer in democracy and the democratic process."

Colonel de Rocque, an aristocrat, had founded a number

of fascist organizations during the 1930s, such as the Croix-de-feu ("Cross of Fire"), before forming an extreme right-wing party. Mitterrand could simply have said that no one is perfect, especially when you are twenty, and that as everyone knew, Colonel de Roque was no more a Nazi than he was anti-Semitic—in fact, he was later deported by the Germans. Everyone would have forgiven Mitterrand his youthful indiscretion. But he wanted to remain forever faithful to the novel of his life. I forgave him. He had spent so much time telling himself stories, whether they were true or not, that he had inevitably ended up believing them.

"I was a product of my environment," he went on, "which was classic petit bourgeois, Catholic, and traditionalist. Therefore conservative. And chauvinistic. But I was not involved in Action Française—the French far right of the time. There was never so much as a shadow of anti-Semitism either in my family or in me. Whenever my mother heard anything against the Jews, she inevitably responded, I remember: 'But have you forgotten? Both Christ and the Virgin Mary were Jews.' My education was completed by the war and captivity. If I do say so myself, from 1942 to 1944 I took a great many risks. I only wish that all the people writing about that period had been with me on the night of November 15, 1943, on that parcel of land flanked on either side by a row of poplar trees, where a tiny plane somehow managed to land for the purpose of bringing me to England. And after we took off the German anti-aircraft really went to town, and God only knows how we made it through that barrage safely. And I also wish that my detractors had been with me roughly three months later, on the night of February 26, 1944, to be exact, when I returned from Great Britain aboard a small craft, which hove to off a coast, the precise location of which none of us knew for sure. They put me into a boat, with a compass and a pair of oars, and pointed shoreward with a 'Row in that direction.' It was pitch black, the sea was extremely rough, and I had no sea legs to speak of. But somehow I made it ashore, and found myself in Brittany."

Suddenly he broke off his story and seized my arm in a tight grip. The memories he had just been evoking seemed to have caused him pain. Was he caught up in nostalgia for things past? At the same time, he felt himself encircled and abandoned. He was dreaming of a night that, at long last, would protect him.

6

$\mathcal{W}$HEN WE WERE BACK beneath the welcoming shade of the trees and settled in our lounge chairs, a well-tanned maitre d' dressed in casual clothes and looking for all the world like a policeman or thinly disguised member of the Secret Service, appeared with a tray filled with foie gras appetizers. As always, because I don't know how to say no and because I've been afflicted since childhood with compulsive overeating, I gobbled a dozen in a row as the president—who had said, "Thank you very much, I think I'll pass"—watched with clear amusement.

I thought I detected the gourmet hand of the president's wife, Danielle. She canned so much foie gras every year that it was impossible to come to Latché, if only for a single meal, without being offered some. I never complained about the seemingly endless supply, for as they say where I come from, it was absolutely tasty, though a trifle starchy—which is always the case for homemade foie gras.

Rather than opening a discussion on the advantages and disadvantages of foie gras, I decided to talk about former president Ronald Reagan, whom Mitterrand had known very well. He looked hard at me and folded his thumb and forefinger into a circle. "Zero," he said. "The man was a nonentity. A complete nonentity."

François Mitterrand was too French to have anything in common with Ronald Reagan, though in general he liked the American president. Like many of his generation, Mitterrand had never forgotten that America had saved his country in two world wars.

But he didn't understand Americans, not because their country was the embodiment of the capitalism he was sworn to fight—Mitterrand was above such notions; the reasons were cultural. For someone who had read widely and deeply, Mitterrand had practically no familiarity with American literature. He was drawn to regional French novels, the literary equivalent of the French ornamental garden, in which everything is neat, controlled, academic. The worlds of John Steinbeck, Mark Twain, or Ernest Hemingway were foreign to him. Only toward the end of his life did he finally discover F. Scott Fitzgerald.

The United States was often the source of our disagreements. Years ago I argued with him about Thomas Jefferson, whom he judged exclusively through the small lens of his private life. Later we quarreled about the assassination of John Kennedy. He maintained it was part of an enormous conspiracy, he was sure of it. He had seen the film three times—Oliver Stone's *JFK,* that is. He knew it by heart.

"It's only a film," I would object.

"Only a film could uncover the truth. Even history itself could not do that."

I didn't count myself as a Reaganite, but my American blood prohibited me from letting him get away with the way he thought about Ronald Reagan, who was to my mind one of many such heads of state throughout history who made up for their lack of native intelligence by the power of their intuition. I reminded the president of the little story Reagan had told me one day back in early 1980, during the New Hampshire primary, when it looked as if he hadn't a chance in hell to win. Virtually everyone was counting him out of the race. "Nobody listens to anything politicians say," he asserted. "When it comes to television, politicians are the last of the last. When one of them rears his or her ugly head during the TV news, sandwiched between a war and an earthquake, it's like a break for the next TV ad: everyone heads for the john. I've figured that much out. So what I do is say the same thing over and over. That way there's a chance, however slim, that people might retain what I say. What's more, I always arrange to appear on TV with some symbolic or picturesque prop next to me, whether it's the stars and stripes, some historical monument, or even a tree. That way, I figure, people might notice me next to the prop."

Mitterrand could not repress a smile, which meant: pretty damn clever.

"You also have to have seen how Reagan wiped out his opponents during the TV debates. I remember one debate in particular, with John Anderson. Somehow, Reagan cajoled Anderson into referring to him throughout the debate as 'Governor,' whereas Reagan always referred to Anderson simply as 'John.' Near the end of the debate, Reagan said in a joking tone and, as I recall, reaching over and putting his hand on Anderson's knee, 'Come now, John, we've known each other for all these years and we've always called each other by our first names. Just because we're on television is no reason not to keep up the old tradition, don't you agree?' Anderson trembled visibly, understanding then and there that he had just been assassinated politically by one swift Reagan jab on national television."

I paused, waiting for the presidential laugh. But there was none.

"Reagan was a dullard," he said. "He kept telling the same stale jokes over and over again, and he never made *any* comment off the cuff. He always had to consult his written notes."

It's true that Reagan was the prototype of the head of state for the twenty-first century: he was as eloquent as his TelePromp-Ter made him, and he was of the species who doubtless hadn't read a book since graduating from college. A man of simple ideas. The anti-Mitterrand.

One of Reagan's former advisers tells the story of how he was assigned to write a major policy speech Reagan was to give before both houses of Congress on the subject of peace in the Middle East. On the appointed day, Reagan dutifully read the first page of the speech, his head lowered, looking for all the world like a chastised canine—that same hangdog look that so besotted the old ladies of the country. "I'm here today to lay out for you," he began, "my fourteen-point plan to reestablish peace in the Middle East." After the first couple of paragraphs, he turned the page, on which he found only a single sentence, in bold letters: "Now, Mr. President, let's see what you can do on your own!"

I'm virtually certain that in such a circumstance Reagan somehow managed to acquit himself more than honorably, whereas greater statesmen would have foundered. Humor was his saving grace. He's a truly modest man, a man so innately humble that he never deigned or needed to lower himself. I fully understand that he had great difficulty in forming any kind of kindred relationship with François Mitterrand, who in the early years of the 1980s took refuge behind his mask—that of a Roman emperor—as he strolled down the corridors of history, censers flanking him on either side.

Ronald Reagan was the kind of statesman who didn't mind if people poked fun at him. It was both his weakness and his strength. There was a famous story about Reagan that Mitterrand had made a point of telling me not once but twice. Happily he refrained from serving it up a third time that day. It was a story about the Cancun summit meeting in 1981, where the heads of state from both the developed and underdeveloped countries had gathered to discuss the fate of the world, especially from the viewpoint of economics. Mitterrand had made a stirring speech, in which he said in essence that if there was ever to be real progress the rich nations would have to truly help the poor, the so-called north would have to support the south. After which Ronald Reagan went to the podium to espouse the opposing view, saying—and I paraphrase—"I'm afraid that I disagree with my distinguished colleague from France. The problem with the Third World is that it lacks what we call the work ethic. I have a close friend in California who owned a tiny parcel of land—arid land that wasn't worth a penny—but he had the incentive to drill for water, and by God! he found water, and turned

that arid land into a thriving farm, and made a good living."
At which point the president of Kenya, Daniel Arap Moi,
exclaimed, "That's extraordinary! Your story reminds me of
my grandfather."

"You see," Reagan said to the distinguished audience,
as if to prove his point. "And tell me, Mr. President, what
happened to your grandfather?"

"He died of starvation," said President Moi, completely
straight-faced.

I was pleased that Mitterrand had spared me that
warmed-over tale, for there's nothing worse than having to
laugh at a story you've already heard several times. It's always a
kind of humiliation. When I was cast in that position with the
president, I always felt that I had been relegated to the low-
liest of the presidential sycophants. I would have preferred to
play the court jester. But in the waning years of any regime,
the court jester had best refrain from telling the truth. The last
thing an aging statesman wants to hear is the truth. He knows
the truth. In fact, the truth is so obvious, so stark, that it gouges
out one's eyes. Which is doubtless why François Mitterrand's
eyes, in those declining months of his administration, looked
so terribly sad.

Since I kept insisting on bringing the conversation,
which tended to fray in the heat of the day, back to Ronald Reagan, the president decided to bring the subject to a
grinding halt. "He was a complete dolt," he said.

Since his mood seemed to be one of candor, I decided
to try and find out what he really thought of a number of
other world leaders, from King Juan Carlos of Spain to Spanish prime minister Felipe González and Mário Soares, the

president of Portugal, but the best I could elicit was that he liked them all yet seemed uninterested in talking about any of them at great length. About former president George Bush he said, with a mixture of nostalgia and ethnocentrism, "He was someone who understood the problems. At bottom, Bush was European. I knew where I stood with him." He also liked President Clinton. "He is very active and sympathetic. The more you know him the better you like him." Mitterrand was fascinated by what he termed Clinton's "animality." He also said that he liked Boris Yeltsin, but I noted that he was more than pleased when I said that I thought Yeltsin was "a thick-skinned brute." But his expression darkened when I added, "This said, I have to admit that he's historically important."

"What do you mean," he said, grimacing, which usually meant he was suffering terrible stomach pains, "when you say 'historically important'?"

"I mean when a political figure and a key political event come together."

"Ah," he said, making even that monosyllabic intonation sound ironic.

"Whenever he came face to face with history, Yeltsin always succeeded in seizing it. In 1987, when he broke with the Politburo. In 1991, when he stood up to the Soviet tanks during the attempted Communist putsch. In complete contrast to Gorbachev, who inevitably managed to let the train of history leave without him."

"And yet, of all the important political figures I met during my two terms in office," Mitterrand objected, "Gorbachev was the most impressive."

"Maybe it was his handshake," I countered. "I can't imagine Ivan the Terrible or Catherine the Great with such a limp handshake. Nor even Kerensky for that matter."

It was Joseph de Maistre[1] who said: "Scratch a Russian and you'll find a Tartar." Yeltsin is a Tartar. Gorbachev's not; he's a European.

Eternal Russia is a horse in need of a strong rider. It loves to "obey," as Balzac once described her, "obey in spite of herself, obey even at the risk of life and limb, obey even when the act of obedience is absurd and offends her deepest instincts." The fact is, Gorbachev wanted to "obey" Russia. Even at the height of his power, he somehow inspired a kind of compassion. You felt a bit sorry for him. In peacetime, he would have made a terrific archduke of Luxembourg. He simply wasn't made for tempests and revolutions. It was written on his face. In times of crisis, his flesh seemed to sag—which the television makeup, which he liked to keep on long after the show was over, failed to mask. And whenever he attacked his political enemies—which he did from time to time more for the form than out of real belief—he was always unconvincing.

What Mitterrand admired about Gorbachev was the reformist, the man who was trying to change communism from within. In 1989, when he and I were discussing Gorbachev, the president had said: "He's a man who has a sense of tradition, but he limits it to Lenin and makes a huge leap over all of Lenin's successors. But it's a sentimental relationship, nothing more. He believes in only four or five of Marx's tenets at most. Otherwise, all he sees are the faults and failings of the Soviet system."

Mitterrand's view of his role in world politics was to act

as a third path between communism and capitalism. It would have legitimized and justified his long years of combat for the socialist cause.

"Do you really think you can accomplish much when you have a limp handshake?" I asked the president.

"He doesn't have a limp handshake," Mitterrand said. "Moist maybe, but not limp."

"What a world of difference between him and Yeltsin," I said. "When Yeltsin enters a room, it's the entire Russian revolution that comes in with him, a massive invasion, massive because of too many potatoes eaten in a single lifetime, red with vodka, his breath reeking so of cabbage soup that everyone in the room is almost felled by it."

Great men are one with their people. When de Gaulle opened his mouth it was France itself speaking, with the tone of a bantering conqueror. He didn't do it on purpose. He *was* France, as Vercingetorix, Hugh Capet, Joan of Arc, or Henry IV had been before him. Historical figures don't lead nations. On the contrary, nations lead them. Nations are in them, dwell within them.

Even when countries see themselves as an empire, or as a race, they are nothing but people. Sometimes they find their double. In the opposite situation, history follows its course, moving with the current downstream. Which is what happened to Russia under Gorbachev. He was content to trot along behind the current of history, the success of which we've all seen.

Gorbachev used to say that history crushes all those who

don't know how to follow it. But it was precisely because he followed it that he was crushed. As Tocqueville said about the ancien régime, by wanting to improve the peoples' lot all it did was make them rise up in revolt. That's what killed Louis XVI: he was always one reform behind the people's demands.

"He would have needed the inner strength of a Luther," I said. "The fact is, he didn't even have that of the pretender pope John XXIII."

The president smiled, his eyes fixed on the tray of foie gras canapés, which I had managed to finish off in less time than it takes to tell. He made no effort to order some more, either because he was lost in his thoughts or because my comments about Gorbachev had offended him. Nonetheless, I decided to pick up the same thread.

"You have to admit," I said, "when all is said and done, Gorbachev was a lightweight."

"He made one serious error of judgment," Mitterrand said. "He thought that a revolution could be stopped in midstream. And it can't. Period."

"You see, you're coming around."

"I had a great many talks with Gorbachev over the years. When I saw him in Kiev in 1989, I advised him to speed up the institutional reform movement and decentralization. He said he didn't see any reason to. He felt the pace at which things were evolving was just fine. His greatest concern was to make sure the unity of the Soviet Union wasn't threatened, and he felt that if he moved any faster it might be. And as you can see, on that score events have proven him right."

Gorbachev did everything in his power to make sure the system did explode. And when it did, one can imagine him saying, as did the king of France when the country was moving toward revolution, I do enough to accommodate my subjects' demands. It's high time now that they do, at least once, what I want.

"You can lay all the mistakes and misjudgments you want at his doorstep," the president said, "but the fact remains, he brought about a bloodless revolution."

"Not quite bloodless," I said.

"True, but virtually bloodless, and that in itself is nonetheless a miracle."

"A mystery is not necessarily a miracle."

I was irritating him. I focused my attention on Baltique; I reached down and petted him in silence.

A caress, even if only to a dog, lightens the air. The president took a deep breath, stood up to go where even the king himself was wont to venture alone. But the president's exit was far from majestic.

7

$\mathcal{B}$ACK FROM HIS TRIP to see a man about a horse, the president popped a juicy grape into his mouth and, without waiting to swallow, began complimenting me on my recent newspaper articles. I knew all too well his methods of wrapping people around his little finger. Till then I had carefully avoided falling into the trap, and in fact I honestly thought I was past that stage in life. To try and make him understand that he was wasting his time, I tried to change the subject, but in vain. When he was off and running, no matter what the subject, there was no stopping him.

Even as life was slowly slipping away from him, the president, enveloped in his pallid shroud of flesh, was still pulling the same old strings. He wasn't complimenting me out of force of habit. It was some deep-rooted pang of anxiety that made him do it. But I was no longer useful to him. In fact, no one was of any use to him. The mind was willing, but the flesh refused to follow. Even as he was praising me in order to seduce me, a mixture of sadness and melancholy was visible in his eyes. He had always looked at the world from on high. Now, at this stage of melancholy, the altitude was no longer measurable. If he hadn't humiliated me by his empty compliments, I doubtless wouldn't have been able to resist going over and hugging him.

"What say we have a bite to eat," he said, getting to his feet, his lips still stained with the juice of the grapes.

Inside, we joined the president's wife, Danielle, who was stretched out in the living room on a lounge chair, her feet swathed in a sea of bandages. She was recovering from a heart operation, and her face showed it: there was something distant in her expression that had never been there before.

"Phlebitis," she said, nodding in the direction of the bandages, the quizzical look on her face indicating that she, like all people seriously ill, couldn't quite understand what was happening to her.

"She's going to be fine," murmured the president. "But I have to say she gave me a terrible scare."

Of the two, however, he was the one who gave real cause for concern. One of the sure signs of approaching death is that the eyes recede deep into their sockets. Mitterrand's face already looked like a death mask. Not so that of his wife.

He was fully aware of that fact. And to make himself forget it, he would constantly laugh. The only problem was, there was not a shred of joy in his laughter. It was forced, almost sad.

When we had taken our seats around the table, the president, almost as if he were apologizing, said, "A friend brought me some lobsters back from Spain. I mean, a *lot* of lobsters, and we simply can't let them go to waste. I only hope you like lobsters."

Before I had time to reply, he began telling me, without the slightest transition, how highly he thought of the new chairman of the Socialist Party, Henri Emmanuelli ("He's really off to a great start, don't you agree?") and from there he moved, again without transition, to an out-and-out attack on his former colleague and ex-prime minister Michel Rocard.[1] Younger and more liberal than Mitterrand, Rocard had become Mitterrand's main rival following the Socialists' victory in 1981, politically as well as morally. Only Rocard could have questioned Mitterrand's sincerity, and for that he was never forgiven. The president reminded me, with intentional malice, that after Rocard had lost his bid to become a member of the European parliament, he had taken up hang gliding.

"You really have it in for poor old Rocard, don't you?" I grumbled.

"Ah," he responded, "I'd forgotten. You two are friends."

His voice, like the high-pitched sound of an electric saw, was filled with mockery.

He shook his head and went on. "You mustn't think I have anything against poor old Rocard. I've never hated the man. He's a decent enough sort. The only thing is, in my view he's simply not up to the jobs he's aspired to. He really is qualified to hold some minor secretarial post in the administration—postmaster general, say, or something similar. But that's all. Haven't events proved me right?"

He searched my eyes, looking for agreement, but found none, so went on. "People often overestimate their own abilities," he opined. "It's as if La Fontaine had aspired to become Aeschylus. There are writers who are talented in one area but insist on writing in a genre that doesn't suit them. Well, that can happen with politicians, too."

Suddenly, he was not only being wrongheaded, but mean-spirited.

His attack on Rocard was perhaps based on the fact that Rocard inevitably gave in to Mitterrand. In fact, I recalled that only a few months before, Mitterrand, referring to Rocard, had said to me, "How in the world could I ever hate someone who has never stood up to me? Oh, maybe once or twice. The first time for a couple of days back in 1981, when we had a major policy difference. And again in 1988, when he was contemplating running for president. All it took me was a forty-five minute breakfast to talk him out of it. No, I have no reason whatsoever to be angry with him."

And for the first time that day, the president's face was wreathed in a sincerely happy smile. But it was a smile not caused by the warmth emanating from the midday earth; it was caused by his blistering attack on Michel Rocard.

"I wish him all the best with his hang-gliding career," he finished off. "I've heard he's got his hang-gliding license. Who knows, he may end up having a glorious second career up there in the wild blue yonder."

The more wickedly cruel he waxed, the older his face looked.

To avoid letting my temper get the better of me, I took a sip of white wine. I always have a good reason for drinking. Sometimes it's because I'm bored. Or because I'm in the midst of an especially fine meal. Or, at times, because I'm afraid of becoming unpleasant. In this instance, I was using the last-named pretense to soothe my troubled conscience. But no, that wasn't the real reason.

I was drinking because it was a lovely, sultry day. That was reason enough.

I emptied my glass, then downed another, at which point I began to feel a pleasant little buzz. Alcohol has always had a positive effect on me: it makes me as docile as a newborn babe. Oh, if I overindulge, I sometimes tend to become a trifle loud, but always in a positive way. Either I flatter, become submissive, or simply become more pleasant. But I hadn't yet reached that stage. Not quite.

The effect of the wine must have showed on my face, for the president began to address me in confidential tones. There was more than a touch of irony both in his voice and his eyes when he said, "Balladur's[2] doing a pretty good job as prime minister, don't you agree?"

"You really think so?"

"He's too perfect, that fellow. So perfect he becomes utterly boring. We'll have to turn over a few Balladur rocks, see if we can uncover a few secret vices."

"Some people already have," Anne Lauvergeon chimed in. "I've heard some nasty gossip that's making the rounds."

"Really?" the president murmured, pausing as if waiting for more details.

Anne refused to take the bait and lowered her head and focused on her plate of lobster. But the president's curiosity was now fully aroused. Like a dog that wouldn't let go of its bone, he went on, "What kind of gossip? What exactly are people saying?"

"Nothing much. The usual inanities," she said.

I felt embarrassed. To ease the growing malaise that was threatening to paralyze the conversation, I tossed a fresh banality into the fray. "One thing you can say about him," I ventured, "he's a real politician."

"With the reservation that he's very thin-skinned," the president said. "He takes very poorly to criticism. And if he's elected president, I guarantee you he'll have problems within the first year of his administration. The French are bored to tears with politics and politicians. If he doesn't produce some tangible results, the people will be marching in the streets, pitchforks in hand, mark my words."

Not all that long ago the president had talked about Balladur in an altogether different way. "You know," he had noted, "I've rarely seen politicians I would rate lower than I rate myself, but he beats all records. So when all is said and done, I can say to myself that I didn't live these last few years in vain. I had the opportunity of meeting someone so coy and bland that I can honestly say to myself—relatively speaking, of course—that I wasn't all that bad. I was, in fact, pretty damn sincere by comparison. If you were to take a knife and lift up his skin, you'd find venom flowing just beneath. Pure venom. He'll betray anyone and everyone, just the way he betrayed Chirac.³ Not that he does it with malice aforethought. He simply can't help it. Betrayal is his middle name. It's part and parcel of his makeup."

When I asked him what he based that low opinion on, the president feigned astonishment. "I don't hate Balladur," he said. "He's a very capable fellow. All I'm doing is portraying him as he really is, nothing more." Then, with a smile, "Each time I take my medicine, I can't help wondering if they're trying to poison me. Shows you the level to which I've descended!"

He laughed, exactly the way he did when he told me about a recent conversation he had had with the prime minister. "I said to him," Mitterrand recounted, " 'The political unrest today reminds me greatly of 1815, when the Duke of Orleans and Louis XVIII were fighting for power.' 'And who, in today's context,' he said, 'would be Louis XVIII?' 'You would,' I said. It was a terrible thing to say, but he simply didn't get it. He thought I'd just paid him a wonderful compliment."

Several years later, when the political scandals of the opposition conservative party were beginning to surface in all their glory, the president had said, only half jokingly but with an inner rage that was ill concealed, "Have you seen what's been going on? All those people are going to fall like tenpins. Before long I'll be the only one left, just wait and see. Even if my health reduces me to a wheelchair. Remember that image of President Roosevelt in his waning days, sitting in his wheelchair at Yalta with a checkered blanket over his knees? I'll be like Roosevelt, and I'll watch as, all around me, politicians fall one by one, like so many flies.

"Edouard Balladur finds himself on the horns of a dilemma. He realizes that several of his ministers are involved in shady affairs, and he can't figure out how to get rid of them. Not all that long ago, during one of our cabinet meetings, he gave me this steely look as if to say, Poor old bastard, you're already half dead. Why don't you just fade away completely and be done with it! Now he can't help but read in my eyes the same message in reverse. He's reached the point that he can't look at me straight in the eye any longer."

Actually, I had the feeling that he didn't dislike or disdain Balladur as much as he pretended. But he needed to vent his hate in order to resist his cancer. His hate was keeping him here on earth. It was his means of survival.

I continued to sip at the wine and let myself slowly metamorphose into a lamb, still unbleating. In my state of bliss, I had more and more trouble following the conversation, which I found moving faster and faster.

I was flying high, and decided there was no way I was going to come down. I was happy just listening passively to the conversation, which did not mean I understood it. And every now and again I made sure to smile. Whenever you find yourself in a social position of weakness, especially with a predator—no matter whether the predator is in a weakened state or not—you must always remember to smile.

The gravest danger, if you find yourself in such a situation, is having to answer a question. Like an unprepared student facing a professor's withering gaze, you quickly turn into a pitiful object. To avoid this danger, feeling completely wiped out as a result of the wine, the heat of the day, and a general sense of well-being, I focused the last vestiges of my attention on the lobster, which was deliciously creamy and fresh, as if it had just been pulled from the sea. I could have sworn it was still quivering. If I understood correctly what the president had been saying, there had been no improvement in Edouard Balladur's unfortunate condition.

Danielle Mitterrand's plate was lobsterless, garnished with only a small piece of grilled meat. Seeing my quizzical look, she explained, "I decided to let you all enjoy the lobsters. I saw them when they were alive, you see. I find it impossible to eat lobster when I've previously seen them alive. I just can't bring myself to do it."

I nodded approval.

"It's unbearable to see a lobster that has just been plunged into boiling water, flailing about with its last bit of strength," she added.

Her husband nodded, not without a certain show of condescension.

I was tempted to remind Danielle Mitterrand of what Pierre Elliott Trudeau, who had then been prime minister of Canada, had said in response to her outrage over the fate of baby seals who were being skinned alive for their pelts in the far north of his country, but I refrained. Trudeau had said: "That may well be, but as for myself, I feel for the poor geese that are force-fed to enlarge their livers and produce foie gras for the French." Nor did I have the courage to respond that as I looked at the piece of meat on her plate I could almost hear the lowing of the cattle as they were being butchered in the slaughterhouse. And I could have commented even further by reminding her that the sausage I had been offered before lunch—which I had politely declined—called to mind the high-pitched squeal of the pigs as they were bleeding to death just before being turned into sausage.

The Greek philosopher and mathematician Pythagoras was a vegetarian. Another Greek, the biographer and moralist Plutarch, said that he failed to understand how people could allow "dead bodies" to be served them at table. Both also remarked that they thought they could actually *hear* the bellowing of the poor beasts as the butcher's sword ended their days. As for that other Greek philosopher, Empedocles, it was his studied opinion that human souls were bound to their bodies as punishment for their crimes, because they had eaten the meat of other creatures.

All these noble thoughts coursing through my mind provided me, at long last, with a subject of conversation worthy of my high-mindedness. Passion quickly swept away the cobwebs that had invaded my brain.

Taking my courage in my hands, I turned to Danielle Mitterrand and said, "I understand you only too well. I'm a vegetarian myself."

"Good for you," she murmured, lowering her gaze to her guilty plate.

Although I don't look down my nose on any kind of succulent poultry, not to mention my serious weakness for foie gras, it would have taken very little convincing for me to espouse the clarion call that Plutarch made almost two thousand years ago. To paraphrase, Plutarch wondered what courage it must have taken the first human to lift to his mouth a piece of raw meat from a just-slaughtered beast, to crush with his teeth the animal's bones; to have been the first person to be served the flesh of corpses that only moments before had been bleating and bellowing, walking and seeing? How could that man have been able to thrust a piece of iron into the heart of a living, feeling fellow creature? How could his eyes have borne the sight of the still-warm, still-quivering bodies?

Since I had only a vague recollection of Plutarch's exact

words on the subject of being a vegetarian, I refrained from trying to quote him exactly and turned instead to Rousseau, closer to home both in time and space, who theorized that man was not really a carnivore, for the simple reason that man possesses both a colon and flat teeth, two key characteristics of the frugivorous order. I felt immediately that I was making not the slightest impression. His mouth filled with lobster, the president gave a smile that very clearly meant, All well and good, but meanwhile all of us here fall into the well-known category of "lobsterivores."

"And then there's this further thought to ponder," Mitterrand murmured between bites. "For all we know, one of us at this very moment may well be eating the Lobster King, the creature who after years of struggle has just seized control of the entire lobster species and whose potentially long and glorious reign we have just nipped in the bud."

The fact was, Mitterrand was far too much of a glutton to appreciate my remarks on the subject of food. Never had I seen him question or hesitate over whatever food had been set before him. On the contrary, he was the kind of person who plunged right in without grace or elegance, with his teeth or his hands, refusing to come up for air until the gleaming porcelain of his plate was once again clearly visible. Apparently he belonged to the same school as Cicero, firmly believing it was far better to die of indigestion than to perish from hunger. I therefore decided it would be an excellent idea to change the subject. It turned, quite naturally, to an assessment of current political figures, not all of whom were execrated. Each time, as had been the case throughout the day when he was feeling good and free of pain, the president offered opinions about several major politicians, including the man who would succeed him as president, and the man who two years later would be named prime minister:

Jacques Chirac: "He's courageous and likable. On a human level, he's perhaps the best of the lot. But there's something irrational about him. Within him. That's why he worries so many Frenchmen."

Lionel Jospin:[4] "What an uptight man! For someone as rigid as he is, he manages to do very well for himself. He's angry with me, but I really like him."

I recalled something that Mitterrand had said about Charles Pasqua, the controversial minister of the interior, some time back. "He's a very solid guy, much steadier on his feet than the other politicians. When he lies, he looks you straight in the eye, and it's you who tremble inside, knowing full well he's lying to you." He said that not with disapproval but with admiration, as though he was talking about another side of himself.

As the waiter served dessert, an apple tart Tatin-style, the president seemed self-absorbed, as he always did at the end of a meal, and began to concentrate on what I call the tooth ritual: he sucked, scratched, and dug with a noise level that would have done credit to a major construction site.

After dessert was over, he went into high dental gear: with a toothpick as tool, he attacked the back molars as well as the old, worn-down canines.

It was painful to behold, watching him there at table with his forefinger probing the inner depths of his mouth. But he hadn't lost his sense of humor. Realizing the spectacle he was making of himself, he shook his head and said, "Can't help it. With me, it's like a profession."

8

*A*S WE WERE HAVING COFFEE outside in the lounge chairs, in the shade of the tallest tree in the garden, Baltique began to pay court to Anne Lauvergeon. Apparently, the presidential bitch had fallen in love with the deputy administrative assistant to the president and was licking her profusely, to her considerable embarrassment. Anne fell silent, as if lost in her thoughts, and though she looked worried, there was a certain irony in her expression, that irony women sometimes display in the presence of a passionate suitor.

And, without question, Baltique's suit could fairly be described as ardent. As time went on, the dog became bolder and bolder. She had begun by rubbing her snout the length of the young woman's leg. After which she had sniffed the lady's hand before searching for something, doubtless an odor, in her armpit, which had not been offered her. Then Baltique began to lick Lady Lauvergeon's neck, her ears, her shoulders, her chin, all of which she yielded without resistance, doubtless by way of sacrificing those pawns in order to guard her Queen, that is her mouth, where she had decided to draw the line.

"Baltique," admonished the president, "stop that. Down, Baltique, down!"

Dogs love me. Often passionately. More than once a dog has mistaken my tibia for a fireplug, without my being the least bit shocked or offended by it. My degree of irritation is generally commensurate with the state of my trouser leg. But till now I had never been the object of canine affection even remotely resembling that currently being lavished on Anne Lauvergeon.

With me, dogs generally spare the preliminaries, getting right down to brass tacks. It took a woman like Anne, proud and puritan, to provoke such ardent transports.

The president couldn't contain his laughter. "She likes you," he said, breaking up. "I only hope you share her feelings."

Anne Lauvergeon would perhaps have been put in an even more embarrassing situation had she not had the presence of mind to slip Baltique a piece of cake, as a diversionary tactic. The dog swallowed it whole and clearly wanted nothing more than another piece as quickly as possible.

Dogs are like everyone else: one pleasure tends to make you forget another, and the sin of the flesh is often superseded by the sin of gluttony, or vice versa. Baltique began to bark. Her libido was quickly forgotten. All she wanted was another piece of cake. Anne Lauvergeon obliged, and Baltique gulped down the new morsel, her tail fanning the warm summer air.

"Don't give her too much," the president warned. "She has a weight problem."

I lay back in my chair and relaxed. If this wasn't happiness, it couldn't be far from it. The warmth of the day filled me with sweet comfort. François Mitterrand, who had also lain back in his chair, his eyes closed, his mouth open, seemed to be in a state of near bliss.

I ruined his serenity when I said to him, "I have never understood why, ever since the liberation, you constantly and unfairly fought General de Gaulle."

The president looked at me askance, his eyes widening. "I simply didn't want to be involved in his power game," he said.

"Is that all Gaullism was, a power game?"

"No, of course not. There was an authentically patriotic aspect of Gaullism. But de Gaulle himself was a control freak. He wanted to dominate everything, pull all the strings. You know, my conflict with de Gaulle stems from the first time I met him, in Algiers on December 2, 1943."

When I asked him whether their conflict wasn't another incarnation of the battle that had been waged throughout Europe during and after World War II, between the resistance forces within a given occupied country and those fighting the Nazis from their refuge outside their respective homelands, I sensed that I had, with that question, regained any territory I had lost with my initial, undiplomatic question.

The president was back on familiar ground and he showed it.

"That's exactly it. If you want to make a rough comparison: in Yugoslavia it was Marshal Tito who led the resistance within his country, who won out over the resistance forces outside Yugoslavia. After the war, the internal resistance therefore took power in Belgrade. In France, the opposite happened. At the liberation, the external resistance completely crushed the resistance forces that had been operating within the country."

"Because the internal French resistance forces didn't have a Tito to oppose de Gaulle."

"Not quite true. It had not one but several Titos. That's why it lost."

"And the antagonism between the two resistances has never ceased since. That's one of the salient points that enables us to understand French politics, from the liberation to this day."

"Absolutely. We who were part of the internal resistance couldn't get along with the external resistants, the Gaullists, whom we looked upon with suspicion."

"Do you ever have any regrets that you weren't a Gaullist?"

"When I arrived in England in 1943, de Gaulle's people said to me: "You'll have the rank of captain, with the corresponding salary. You'll take the resistance name of Monnier. But first of all you have to sign this paper committing yourself to the Free French forces." To which I responded, "Me? Sign a paper? Never!" Nevertheless, I was made a captain and did take the name of Monnier. But I'm one of the two people—I don't know who the other is—who refused to take any military pay from the Free French forces. My stipend was duly recorded on the books but I never took it out. My interest on the principal has mushroomed over the past fifty years: several years ago someone reminded me that I was owed a rather princely sum."

"Why did you take such a radical stand vis-à-vis de Gaulle?"

"I didn't want to become involved in somebody else's political adventure. I didn't want to owe allegiance to anyone."

"What you're saying in essence is, you became an anti-Gaullist because you were afraid they would somehow control you. Was that the only reason?"

"De Gaulle had a strategy of eliminating anyone and anything that might prevent him from becoming master of France. For example, all the heads of the various internal resistance movements whom he summoned down to Algeria never returned. They were made members of different Free French committees of one thing or another, and were never heard from again."

"De Gaulle didn't prevent you from coming back to France, though."

"I was a comparatively minor section head compared to the others. Despite that, it took a lot of doing before I did manage to return. It's true that my meeting with de Gaulle went very badly. He wanted to get his hooks into me, don't you see. When I went to see him in his villa, which was called 'Les Glycines' — 'Wisteria' — he received me very cordially. De Gaulle was an extremely courteous man. He said to me, 'I've worked out a plan to provide aid to the French POWs. We have the financing and a plan for parachuting arms to certain elements. But before we implement the plan, it's essential that the various POW organizations inside France join forces. At present there are three such organizations. In my view, that's two too many. They should be merged into one.' I responded that I too felt the need to unify and coordinate all the POW efforts. He went on, 'Your leftist organization, and the one led by Monsieur Charette, have to come together into a single group.' 'Ah, yes,' I said, 'Monsieur Charette. You mean your nephew.' Charette was de Gaulle's sister's son. A man I didn't like, and who liked me even less. De Gaulle wouldn't relent, pressing his demand as insistently and as often as he could. 'And once you've joined forces,' he went on, 'the newly merged POW committee will be headed by Monsieur Charette.' 'I'm afraid that's out of the question,' I protested. 'And why is that?' de Gaulle wanted to know. 'Because neither I nor any of the leaders of the other POW organizations will agree to back a leader we don't feel is qualified, and whose authority we don't recognize.' After I got back to Paris I did meet with the other groups, and we did merge them into a single entity, but greatly to my advantage. My organization had fifty percent of the voting power in the new group, and all the other POW groups shared the other fifty percent."

"That can't have helped cement your relations with de Gaulle."

"No, obviously not. But don't get me wrong: I never hated General de Gaulle. I'm not that crazy. It's not as if I had a fixation on the man. I have managed to focus on a few other subjects from time to time."

"I gather you saved his life at one point, kept him from falling out of the window of the Paris city hall at the liberation."

"Oh! That's a minor incident, though it happens to be true. Just after the liberation a huge crowd gathered outside the city hall, to hail the conquering heroes. To greet the crowd, de Gaulle climbed up onto the windowsill (there was no balcony) of the prefect's office, and threw both arms into the air in a sign of victory. When he. appeared, the people weren't exactly sure who they were seeing—General de Gaulle or General Leclerc—so while some shouted "Long

live de Gaulle," others were shouting, "Long Live Leclerc."[1]
At that point, there was a great jostling of the people in the
prefect's room, and de Gaulle almost lost his balance. It so
happened that I and someone else were standing just behind
de Gaulle. We grabbed and held onto his legs, which probably saved him from plunging into the void. That's all there
is to the so-called story. I saw him the next day at the Defense Ministry, where the first cabinet meeting of the new
government was held. I remember I was wearing sneakers,
which were the only shoes I owned. De Gaulle went around
the room, shaking hands with everyone and engaging them
in small talk. When he came to me, the youngest man in the
room, he looked at me and said, with more than a trace of
malice, 'You again!' At which point I knew that, whatever
my political fortunes might be, de Gaulle would not be an
ally."

"And after that, you never saw him again?"

"No, I did see him many years later, in 1958, just before he took power again, when he summoned the rank-
ing members of all the political parties, big and small, to the
Laperouse Hotel, to announce his plans. I got up and gave
a speech attacking his coup d'état, which I'm sure displeased
him greatly. After that, our paths never crossed again."

Which wasn't quite true. De Gaulle's and Mitterrand's
paths crossed countless times thereafter, as each fought to
preserve his place in history.

Vercingetorix found himself facing the Roman conquerors.
Joan of Arc had the English to deal with. De Gaulle had the

Nazis. Mitterrand had no one. And that was his problem in relation to history.

"Was there a love-hate factor in your relationship with de Gaulle?"

"Not at all. Our differences were exacerbated when it became apparent to him that there was some vague possibility I might succeed him. But I did nothing to keep that dispute alive."

"Come, come now. The easiest way to get your back up is to mention his name in your presence."

"It's not de Gaulle himself that gets my back up, it's the veneration, the false devotion he inspires. My protest isn't against de Gaulle, it's against a false god."

"Nonetheless, it must be hard to be president of France after de Gaulle. Even after all these years, he still casts a very long shadow. I'm sure you must find it unbearable."

"I've never had any problem living with that shadow."

Wrong. Mitterrand wanted to do away with that shadow, or that major historical blemish. The problem was, the damn spot wouldn't come out. And that infuriated him. I remember something he had told me several years before on the subject. "I never dwell on de Gaulle," he had said, "but from time to time I encounter his image. Often in a positive way. De Gaulle was above all a strategist, not a politician with far-seeing ideas. If you put aside his insistence on France becoming a nuclear military power—and after all he was a soldier by profession—he never understood the importance of Europe, of this continent conceived of as a single entity. He also never understood the problems of the Third World, nor did he comprehend the importance of scientific research. It's true that he did understand the importance of ending colonialism, but that came very late in his career; it took him a very, very long time to do something about it. And every time he changed positions, he made a theory out of it. So it was that he ended up espousing all sorts of causes and situations that he never really wanted to."

De Gaulle made such a mark on the twentieth century that he left behind him clouds of political dust, and the echoes of his whinnying voice still reverberate down the corridors of history many years after his death. People like de Gaulle never die.

Often, statesmen who think they are occupying the center stage of world politics have already been dead for a long time. As for General de Gaulle, he outlived his life. His message is still with us, buzzing in our ears, coming to us from the afterlife.

De Gaulle wasn't afraid of dying because he knew that he would die only long after his physical demise, very long thereafter. That is why he was amused rather than terrified by the various attempts against his life.

A year before he died, he had said to his friend and longtime collaborator André Malraux: "You know, courage always consists of not paying any attention to danger. The way to die is to be assassinated or struck down."

Mitterrand, on the other hand, was afraid to die because, in contrast to de Gaulle, he wasn't France but just another Frenchman. Since he had never lived far from the day-to-day world, he was afraid of falling. He was afraid of the yawning void that awaits us all. He was like you and me. He wasn't a hero.

Therefore, whenever he had the chance, he did his best to cut de Gaulle down to size. He didn't do it on purpose. Posterity is nothing more than managing to make history's honors list. Get your name in the history textbooks. He knew that all too well, and it worried him. The thought that he might become the contemporary equivalent of Louis the Pious, who succeeded Charlemagne, haunted him, as did the notion that he might somehow end up in the dustbin of history, a boring footnote.

Whatever his merits, there was no reason to believe he had been an outstanding president. Actually, there were many reasons to believe he had been forcibly run-of-the mill, because of the times in which he ruled. That's why his face clouded over, seemed somehow sad whenever de Gaulle's name came up. When the conversation turned to his illustrious predecessor, his tone of voice changed, as if he was overwhelmed by a wave of weariness.

"People often talk about de Gaulle's views on Algeria, and most of what they say is nonsense," he went on. "They conveniently forget that after the insurrection of 1945 he ordered the bombardment of Sétif, which resulted in the death of 45,000 souls. You have to admit that that's far worse than my having made the mistake of saying at one point, 'Algeria is France,'[2] which I've been castigated for ever since."

"Would you say that de Gaulle was reactive rather than proactive when it came to Algeria? That events led him rather than his being in charge?"

"He played with events. Toyed with them. He was very

clever, but also very cynical. If I had been a fraction as calcu-
lating, can you imagine the reproaches I would have had to
endure? But whenever people talk about de Gaulle's political
stance vis-à-vis the Third World, they conveniently forget that
aspect. As they gloss over the speech he made about Phnom
Penh." He gave a profound sigh, as if discouraged. "When all
is said and done, de Gaulle was a man very much behind the
times."

"Not on the social level?"

"There, too."

He gave me a withering look, sighed again as if to indi-
cate how irritated he was either by my ignorance or my lack
of sincerity, and said, "What's come over you anyway?" Then
after a pause, "In 1958 de Gaulle was forgiven for his 1940
rebellion by submitting completely to the will and wishes of
the bourgeois leaders of the country, the conservative forces."

"Still, by setting up the Fifth Republic he gave France a
new lease on life. A breath of political fresh air."

"His government was nothing but a succession of trag-
edies. He had to dissolve parliament after having antagonized
some of his most faithful supporters over the question of European unity. Then he requisitioned the miners before doing a
180-degree about-face on the subject. Which was the right
decision, by the way. It showed among other things that he
could be extremely malleable. He displayed that same flexibil-
ity again in 1967 when he let it be known that he intended
to devaluate the franc, then suddenly changed his mind. Not
to mention that bizarre incident in 1968, when everything
was going to hell in a handbasket around him, when he
took off for Baden-Baden. I could go on about that at great

length, but—and I'm sure this will shock you—I'll let it go at that."

"Do you have the distinct feeling that people gloss over or forgive de Gaulle more things than they do other politicians, than they forgive you, to be precise?"

"As far as I'm concerned, it's only normal that people take me to task for everything I do, every move I make. That's because I'm still here, still in power. That's the only reason. Later on, we'll see."

There was a moment of silence, then the president suddenly said, in an outburst that was clearly heartfelt, "When it comes to de Gaulle, people rewrite history."

"Do you deny that he was an extremely important figure in contemporary history?"

"Not at all. He had two or three moments of grandeur. One was the eighteenth of June 1940, another was when he had the intuition to put an end to the Fourth Republic, change the constitution, and start the Fifth. And he also had the flair to insist on France's becoming a nuclear power, as a force of defense."

"That's not too shabby."

"True, it's not that bad a record. I've never said it was. De Gaulle is a major figure in the history of France, but from there to treat anyone who takes issue with anything he said or did as a heretic . . ."

"After having fought him so long and so hard, the fact is you did take up the General's cudgels in the areas of French institutions, national defense, foreign policy."

"Took up his cudgels! That's hardly the way I'd phrase it. I didn't govern the way he did. When I didn't like a tribunal

I didn't simply up and dissolve it. Nor did I ever say, as he did at one juncture, that all power flowed from the presidency, including the judiciary. During my administration, television and radio were freed from the yoke of political control. When you come right down to it, democracy made de Gaulle suffer. It made me suffer, too, but I got used to it."

At which point he laughed wholeheartedly, his laughter rising to mingle with the birdcalls above, in the gentle afternoon.

His hand moved in search of Baltique, either to caress her or be caressed, who knows, and the look on his face was that of a man who has just had the last word. Then he said, almost as an afterthought, "Relations between de Gaulle and me were always strange. As long as he was alive, I was always in pursuit of him in one way or another. Then, after he died, he's been the one pursuing me."

It was only normal. De Gaulle was still among us. The realists, with their cynicism and sniggering laughter and political wheeling and dealing, are quickly forgotten. Others, like de Gaulle, who really cared about their country, who were in a sense its conscience, generally endure, even if they frequently give the complacent middle class indigestion.

That day, there was nothing at all wrong with our digestion. I doubt that anything or anyone could have upset it. It was because of the sky overhead that blended with, no, became one with us.

9

A FAT LAZY FLY, with the same blue glints of and mannerisms as a helicopter, was buzzing about, as if deciding which target it would choose. Apparently I was its choice, and it circled me as if I was a corpse, settling from time to time on my lips, on the tips of my eyelids, as if preparing to feast on those choice parts of my body. Even as I was lifting my hand to chase it away it had already made its getaway.

I've always been a target not only for flies but for mosquitoes as well, which love me and make my summers unbearable. I remember especially one summer in Canada, when I was tramping through the forests of northern Ontario, with clouds of mosquitoes in my wake that, periodically, would swarm down and pounce on me, leaving me covered with painful welts.

This particular fly was also enamored of François Mitterrand. Since his mouth was often open, either because he was speaking or because his lips were lightly parted when he was listening, I was afraid that the fly, during one of its several incursions on or near the president's mouth, would inadvertently slip inside.

But maybe I was wrong: maybe the fly flitting endlessly

back and forth between us was really a kind of stage director, signaling whose turn it was to speak, bringing us ever closer together.

But for the moment the president was not in a speaking mood. He was a man who savored silence. In fact, as long as I've known him he had never truly enjoyed talking. I'm said to be a man of few words myself, and he and I have spent many long hours in days gone by in a train compartment or in the back seat of a car together, without so much as exchanging a single word, each of us lost in our own thoughts. It was a game we played: whoever was the first to speak, lost. Inevitably, he was the winner. Now, once again, I was the first to yield.

"When you hear someone say that you are going to leave the Socialist Party in the same condition you found it, what's your reaction?"

"That's a poor joke," he said. "There will come a day when the Socialists, who have not had a good word to say about me recently, will miss me, you'll see."

When I asked him whether he thought socialism could make a political comeback, he narrowed his eyes as if concentrating on the question and said, "After the fall of communism, socialism went through a real crisis in the wake of all the confusion surrounding that momentous event. All of a sudden, all the grand Socialist theoreticians seemed wrong or hopelessly out of date. I think that blanket condemnation is erroneous. But that's the way of the world. When things don't go according to plan, then the whole kit and caboodle is to blame."

"Aren't there other reasons the electorate has turned away from socialism?"

"Of course there are. More than a decade of being in power. That in itself is a major factor. Furthermore, we Socialists were used to being the opposition party. We weren't used to wielding power. In 1982, after we first came to power, we didn't have enough trained staff, sufficient cadres to administrate properly the various departments and ministries. There are a lot of people who blame our party's lack of unity. But what really hurt us politically was the accumulation of mediocre scandals that has beset us over the years, which has made people question the honesty and morality of the party."

"What people refer to as the breakdown of the Left's morality?"

"At the same time these affairs were uncovered, the opposition was relentless, conveniently forgetting the parable about the mote and the beam—'why beholdest thou the mote that is in thy brother's eye, but considerest not the beam that is in thine own eye?' If you make a quick count, which might seem a ridiculous exercise, you'll note that far more conservative than liberal politicians have been either accused or indicted. Which doesn't excuse anyone. The fact is, the Socialists who have been incriminated were wrong to do what they did. But the electorate is far harsher and more demanding when it comes to the Left than it is with the Right. Voters were shocked when members of our party turned out to be less than honorable. And they were right. The voters let us know how they felt at the polls."

The president waved away the venturesome fly that had lighted on his forehead; the intrepid insect then swooped down onto my forearm, remaining there just long enough to feast on its desired ration of my sweat.

"The Socialists will return to power some day," he went on. "Not in my lifetime no doubt, for as you know my days are numbered. But it will happen sooner than you think."[1]

"The Communists themselves, who were politically dead a few years ago, are making a comeback in Eastern Europe."

"Who would ever have predicted that?" he said, feigning astonishment.

"But under different political names and different agendas."

"True. It's not as if they're coming back with their same old shopworn programs, and that's all to the good."

"You know the story about the Russian worker who comes home one day to his apartment on the twenty-seventh floor of his building and turns on the electricity. To his great surprise, the lights come on. 'Good god,' he says, 'the Communists must be back in power.'"

A pained smile, more out of courtesy than conviction.

"A funny story," he said, "but it isn't true. One thing you can say about communism is that it wasn't efficient."

"The reason the Soviets always prevented Westerners from traveling into the more remote regions on the country was not, as they proclaimed, out of a concern for national security. It was because they didn't want outsiders to see what a sorry mess the country was in. They didn't want them to see communism in its day-to-day reality: people dressed in rags, with not enough to eat. They didn't want them to see the haggard look on people's faces. If they had, the fear factor would have been dispelled, and fear was one of the Soviets' trump cards in dealing with the West."

"All power reposes on fear," the president observed. "More or less."

"But especially in dictatorships. A few months before the official fall of communism, I visited the Soviet military base at Cronstadt. You can't believe the sorry state it was in: the barrier gate at the entrance to the camp was missing, the sentry box was tilting dangerously off center, the whole camp was a glorified garbage pit. Once you had seen that, there was no way you could any longer believe in the superiority of the Red Army. Glasnost had done the system in: by eliminating the fear factor, Gorbachev had driven in the last coffin nails of communism."

He nodded. I couldn't tell whether it was out of fatigue or because he agreed with what I had said. Maybe both, the way you do when you nod in agreement to the person speaking when you're bored by his or her conversation. I cursed myself for having bored this man who, nearing the end of his life and far from well, deserved better.

There was a long moment of silence, then the president made me a gift of one of those pithy verities he loved so dearly: "Communism and socialism are two branches of the same tree. The way Christianity and Islam are."

A few years ago, when I asked him whether he was proud of having been the liquidator of the Communist Party, François Mitterrand stiffened visibly, as if I had just insulted him, then said, "I didn't set out to 'liquidate,' as you put it, the Communist Party. I was simply trying to further the Socialist cause."

"You used the Communist Party for your own needs, then cast it aside."

"I made no effort to resist the attempt to unify the Left. Politically, it was inevitable. I did nothing to block it. Period."

"But you can't deny that, politically, you benefited enormously from that unification."

"That's true. When I took over the Socialist Party in 1971, all the cities controlled by the Socialists in the Nièvre department[2] were supported by the heads of local businesses, all of whom were anti-union. The unification of the Left gave us credibility, which had been eroded by that political compromise. As did our joint political platform. Those two elements—unification and clear political agenda—enabled us to win back the liberal voters."

"After all the many years you've been in power, do you think the liberal voters are still with you?"

"I've always remained faithful to my Socialist convictions. When I came to power in 1981, I was faced with a choice between Lenin or social democracy. I opted for the latter, always trying to keep in mind France's special needs within that context. This said, I also had to cope with the dominant—and dominating—forces of French society, which means business and banking, both of which were historically and politically opposed to everything we stood for. What frightens and upsets me today is that what we viewed then as a compromise, to get the country moving forward, other people now view as a theory."

"But isn't social democracy a theory?"

"It's a necessity. The dominant elements of society are just that: dominating. That we wanted to alter or control them changes nothing of the basic equation. They are there, immutable, and they must be dealt with. To reform them is a very delicate and complicated process."

"But what you call the dominant elements of society ended up supporting you, as you supported them."

"I allowed them to survive. But it cost me dearly to see that things didn't work out the way I had hoped or planned."

"Are you sorry you weren't more heavy-handed?"

"Of course not. Force is never the best way. When you impose the rule of force, you inevitably bring down democracy, and ultimately you resolve problems in ways that commonly end in bloodshed. Without abandoning any of my basic principles, I believe I have governed in such a way that, during both my terms of office, there was a greater feeling of unity—of 'togetherness,' to use that overworked term—than there was during de Gaulle's tenure. Under de Gaulle, there may have been consensus but there was no open discussion, no give-and-take, which God knows there has been during my presidency. And I must say I'm proud of that."

He had delivered that same little speech to me one day years before, in his office at the Elysée Palace, and there was something haughty about his delivery, the son of Caesar posing for history. Since then, the approach of death had brought him down from his pedestal. He had divested himself of his imperial bearing and once again become himself, that is, what we all are: very little in the greater context of things.

Some time after our meeting at the Elysée, when I asked him how he defined socialism, he had replied: "When someone asked the same question of Harold Wilson, who was then prime minister of England, he answered: 'It's a science.' I find it harder to summarize socialism in a single phrase. But if I was obliged to, I think I'd say: It's a system of justice. In the strict sense of the term. Or I might be tempted to say: It's a city. In other words, an effort to bring about a kind of urban solidarity. But even as I say that, I don't find it adequate. In any case, what one can say in all fairness is that socialism is the struggle for life, for the right of the poor and downtrodden to share in the fruits of their efforts."

"Which means that you see a future for socialism?"

Which led to another of his spontaneous aphorisms: "There's always a future for those who think ahead, who focus on the future."

"Yes, but what assurance is there that socialism, which is a product of nineteenth-century thinking, will last forever?"

"None, to be sure. But the fact remains that the competition between the classes in positions of power and authority and those moving up the social ladder has not disappeared since the last century."

"What you're describing is the definition of the Left rather than socialism proper."

"In the nineteenth century, whenever one spoke of resistance, it was the conservatives voicing their concern about the so-called lower classes. On the other side, there was the movement, that is the efforts, by those at the base of society to improve their lot. The reality of industrial society soon showed that that 'movement'—the struggle for human justice, for progress—was identified with socialism."

"You sound very much like the philosopher of radicalism, Alain,[3] who once said, 'Nothing is more dangerous than an idea, when it's the only one we have.' When all is said and done, don't you feel more like a radical than a Socialist?"

"Not at all! I don't feel at all like a radical. I'm a Socialist who detests sectarianism and who believes that any idea has to be mulled over in one's head a hundred times, and if necessary modified, before being put into practice. And socialism presupposes structures; its policy or policies can never be replaced by a moral or simply by an ideal. That pragmatism is what above all distinguishes a Socialist from a radical. Which doesn't mean that both shouldn't join forces in the movement."

He had the look of a visionary about him as he uttered that last statement, as if he had just spoken a cosmic truth, when I paraphrased the maxim by André Frossard about the real point of being a Leftist being that when you come to power, you can govern like a conservative to your heart's content. Mitterrand didn't seem to find that funny, nor did he even react to the point of favoring me with a disapproving frown. I had a feeling I had hurt him.

The president sank back deeper into his chair. It was his way of retreating from the relentless onslaught of pain, which was becoming increasingly intrusive. Within him, pain was settling in, already feeling more and more at home. It dwelled within his body. It obsessed him to the point where there were times he could think of nothing else. And, in conjunction with the repeated assaults of the fearless fly, it aroused the wrath that had been lurking inside him unexpressed. It was that pain that twisted his mouth into a grimace as he said, "At the time of the Popular Front in the 1930s, people talked about the 'Two

Hundred'—the two hundred families that wielded all the real power in France. The expression was a trifle too neat, I admit, too pithy, but it was basically accurate. Today the situation is quite different. What we're seeing more and more is an enormous concentration of wealth and power, not in individuals but in conglomerates, major corporate mergers where financial capitalism is taking over from business—and that includes big business. Entrepreneurs are giving way to those who control the financial markets. The privatizations taking place worldwide are only speeding up the process. I see this as a clear and present danger for our society. Entrepreneurs, who by definition have to be aware of and sensitive to social considerations, are fast becoming an endangered species."

"And what do you see as the consequences of this change?"

"This evolution in my view is going to have several serious social implications. The head of a company cannot ignore his or her personnel. Today, financiers have no such qualms. They have only one concern: results, return on investment, which means the bottom line. And a bottom-line mentality is a dire threat to the social fabric. Financiers, for instance, couldn't care less about the social effects—the human factor—of downsizing. When a company downsizes, with hundreds and perhaps thousands of lives disrupted or even ruined, its stock inevitably goes up. It's a different mentality altogether."

At this point he was speaking very quietly, like someone husbanding his remaining strength, saving it for the final breath, and I couldn't help wondering how he could go on discussing the dangers of capitalism when he knew that death was lurking just around the corner and, what was more, he was being harassed by a fat fly.

Bossuet, one of France's major prelates and orators, would have loved to die in the midst of delivering a sermon. The master chef Brillat-Savarin would gladly have given up the ghost as he was concocting a chocolate truffle. Charles Sanson, the executioner during Louis XIV's reign, after an execution. Baudelaire, in his artificial paradise, after finishing a poem. François Mitterrand, it would appear, apparently aspired to render his soul as he was railing against the big bosses. It was his way of denying death.

Everyone would like to die the way Molière did, on stage, where death caught him by surprise. When death comes upon you while you're going about your daily business, it's nothing more than one more incident along the path of life. It's easier to accept, for it's no longer the full stop—the finality—that you've been dreading or anticipating for weeks on end, stretched on your bed of pain. It has become no more than a natural phenomenon.

The president wanted to die the way he had not lived: naturally, like all other common mortals. But he had already accepted what lay ahead, so much so that at times he even forgot to swat at the hovering fly.

A Spanish proverb says that flies never alight on a pot that's boiling. He—Mitterrand—was not boiling. Nor was I. I felt as pleasantly lukewarm as the grass around us.

10

*I*T WAS AS IF SOMETHING had eaten away at his face from within. There was nothing left but the skin, and that was transparent. Beneath that skin lay the void, which would soon have its way. That was why, I suspected, his eyes sometimes suddenly opened wide, as if he was terrified.

He had been reduced to being an actor playing the role of his own life, an actor who couldn't find a way to exit gracefully from the stage. He couldn't even find it in him to fend off the fly. He must have read my thoughts, for suddenly he got to his feet and said, "What do you say to another walk in the woods?"

I imputed his move to the fly. He couldn't bring himself to kill it. He preferred to run away from it, as he was running away from death.

"I'm going to stop off at the sheepfold to fetch a cane," he said. "I don't really need it, but you never know when it might come in handy." His smile was almost childlike before he went on. "I also need to fetch my cap. At my age, a cap is always a good idea."

The sheepfold was exactly the same as I remembered it: one large, round room, filled with shelves on which was perched a substantial collection of pocket books. The bed was set squarely in the center of the room, doubtless to remind one that it was, despite its modesty, the most important piece of furniture there. Despite its name—for it had at one point housed the farm's sheep—it was the presidential bedroom.

He tried on several caps, then headed off for his new constitutional, with Anne Lauvergeon, Jacques Pilhan, and me in his wake.

The air was limpid. The midday sun had chased away the last vestiges of humidity, which had been absorbed into the air. And yet the air was "dirty" because it was swarming with flies and insects. At certain spots, especially beneath the trees, the clouds were so thick they formed a brownish-gray mass.

"People constantly question your sincerity," I said. "In fact, lots of people claim you're not even a Socialist at heart."

I could see I had touched a nerve. "You can't be serious! Not only was I head of the Socialist Party for a good ten years, but I was always the target of any and all attacks against Socialists and socialism because of my position! I've been a confirmed Socialist for thirty-five years, and I've never deviated one iota from that conviction."

"But people are convinced that in your heart of hearts you're really a European," I insisted.

"What short memories people have from one generation to another! I was born during one world war and I fought in the next. What a mountain of massacres, of wanton death and destruction! And of course I learned from those hard lessons of history. Today I'm one of the few survivors of the First

European History Congress, which was held in 1948 in The Hague, presided over by Winston Churchill. I've continued the struggle ever since."

It was siesta time. The wind was asleep. The forest was a panoply of peace. All I wanted was to sit down on a sandy slope and abandon myself to the happiness of the moment, but the president was walking briskly, as if in a hurry to get wherever he was headed.

"Were you ever concerned that France would lose its identity, or have it sorely diminished, in the context of a European community?"

"You sound like a nationalist," he said. "That's the way they all talk, and I can tell you they don't give a damn about France's precious identity."

"Or maybe they care too much about it."

"Wrong. Either they don't care enough or they don't care at all."

"André Malraux once observed that de Gaulle was bearing on his broad shoulders the corpse of France, while pretending to the world that it was alive and well."

"France was never dead. Or if it was, as may have been the case in 1870 and again in 1940, it somehow always managed to raise itself again from the dead."

His eyes had brightened. He was more than fond of aphorisms, which prompted me to remind him of what the Catholic writer Georges Bernanos once said about Bonaparte when the latter was interned at Saint Helena: "Napoleon bragged that he had taken advantage of imbeciles. But eventually, it was the imbeciles who took advantage of Napoleon." It was they who dreamed up this stupid legacy called nationalism that still has a trickle-down effect on, and sullies, France to this day.

"Nationalism," the president said grimly, "is the opium of imbeciles."

"Why didn't you ever come out and say that publicly?"

"In politics, it's best not to speak ill of imbeciles."

Several months later, however, in a speech he delivered before the European parliament in Strasbourg, he did come out and say it, in very strong terms. "Nationalism," he said, "is tantamount to declaring war."

Suddenly he stopped in his tracks, stared directly at me, his lips slightly parted, and for a moment I thought he was going to give me a bear hug. "After all these years," he said, "I'm really happy we have a chance to talk again."

"Yes," I said, slightly embarrassed and not quite sure how to respond, "I'm happy too." When we had resumed our walk, I decided to broach the subject of Germany. "One talks a lot about the 'German question.' But you can't blame Germany for being so big. Still, don't you find that it weighs a bit heavily on the rest of Europe?"

"We have to face the fact that Germany does exist. It represents a great people who are in the midst of a major evolution. We happen to be that country's next-door neighbor, and that proximity has not always been easy. Ever since Bouvines[1] in the thirteenth century, we've had to face up to that reality. It's my view that we've had quite enough of confrontation! Better learn to get along, which is what we're trying to do when we talk about a unified Europe."

"We should take advantage of the opportunity while we

still have German chancellors who are European-minded. I have the feeling that the present chancellor, Helmut Kohl, is more European than German. Am I wrong?"

"He's a native of the Rhineland, therefore someone who is oriented toward the West. I like him a lot, and he returns the feeling."

"I know. In his office in the chancellery there are only two photographs. One is of Konrad Adenauer, who was his spiritual father, and the other is of you, the photograph you inscribed to him."

"I've never understood why people have so often tried to picture him as a blithering idiot."

"Maybe because he stutters."

"He has an enormous amount of common sense, he's as tenacious as they come, and he's a man of great authority."

"Because he was in power when the unification of Germany took place, there's no doubt he'll go down as one of the most important political figures of the last half of the twentieth century. He has to know that, yet it's never gone to his head. He also has humor. Once when I was interviewing him and we were talking about his place in history, he said, 'When I wake up during the night I never think about my place in history. I think about going into the kitchen and raiding the refrigerator.'"

"He's a colorful figure, a man who knows how to turn a mean phrase. But don't fool yourself, he's also a man full of self-doubt, who's ridden with anxiety. I often call him on the phone for no special reason, just to chat or find out how he is. I enjoy talking with him, and when I sense he's in a self-doubting mood, I do my best to cheer him up."

"You should have called him a bit more often during German reunification."

"Don't bring up that old chestnut again!"

If there hadn't been that cheerful note in his voice, I wouldn't have known whether he was joking or serious when he said that. It was an old discussion between us. In 1989 Mitterrand had done his best either to prevent or delay German reunification after the Berlin Wall had come down, whereas France's historical mission at the time should have been to encourage unification. De Gaulle had called for it earlier on, as had Renan[2] a century before. When History becomes ineluctable and transcends us, wisdom dictates that those in power should at least pretend to be the instigators of change.

One day years earlier I had said to the president, "You were wrong to try and slow down the course of history. Both Gorbachev and Kohl were right when they said, a few months before the Wall came down, unification was like the Rhine: there was no way you could stop its flow."

"My view was that we needed to impose certain conditions on Germany before agreeing to unification."

"Since the end of World War II, Franco-German friendship was never based on any kind of ratio of relative military strength. Never."

"That may be," the president said, "but Germany is a strange country that has no fixed boundaries, especially in the East. I felt strongly they should be clearly spelled out before unification was allowed to take place."

He was right. Germany is a kind of enormous jelly-fish that hovers over the Old World. Just when you think it's veering in one direction, it moves off in another. Actually, Germany isn't a state in the true sense of the term; rather it's a people. And it has spawned others in its image all over the world. Even in Russia. A people that isn't really a nation is inevitably a threat to world peace.

I thought François Mitterrand's stance on German unification was wrong at the time, but his sin was venial. Germany itself soon forgot the offense. When anyone criticized or attacked French political strategy at the time in Kohl's presence, the German chancellor inevitably bristled. Several days after my conversation with Mitterrand I heard Kohl say, "How could I be angry with the French president? He's the man who, as far back as 1983, came to my defense when it was a question of letting the Americans install their Pershing missiles on German soil, to counter the Russian SS 20 missiles. He gave a key speech in the Bundestag that year that helped make it happen. His support was some of the most important anyone has given me in the course of my term as chancellor."

Forgotten was Mitterrand's anti-Kohl stance six years later. Not only forgotten but forgiven. Mitterrand, the master statesman, had executed a few leaps and pirouettes and once again landed squarely on his feet.

A photographer appeared out of nowhere: Jean-Jacques Cecarini. He was sweating blood, for he knew that the president did not like having his picture taken, especially these days, and the man knew he had only two or three minutes to complete his assignment.

The president removed a stray hair from my jacket, then turned to pose for the camera, saying, "We can call this picture: The Infernal Couple Together Again At Last."

He reached over again and straightened my collar, which was crooked. It was a gesture of friendship, an almost feminine gesture, and I was touched by it. Again I felt like giving him a fraternal hug, but refrained.

When the photographer had finished his shoot, I went back to the German question. Was he worried about the future of Franco-German relations?

"There will always be crises," he said. "One day Willy Brandt said to me, 'Soon there will be one chancellor for all of Germany, and only one.' But perhaps he was being too pessimistic." Mitterrand smiled, at no one in particular. "Schmidt and Kohl have both belied that prediction. I hope their successors manage to do the same."

He stared intently into the forest, like a dog stalking its prey, then murmured, "Don't you have the feeling sometimes that the ocean is in the forest?"

"For me, all forests are oceans. They sleep, they sometimes roar or bellow like the ocean waves. Except, in the first instance, there's no one around to say it."

He liked it when I mouthed platitudes. He looked pleased. I was pleased that he was pleased.

We all walked along for quite some time, saying nothing. I profited from the silence and inhaled the forest air. I wanted to retain a bit of the pure air in my lungs, which it gently tickled, like a fond memory.

Suddenly the president slowed down to let Anne Lauvergeon, who was wearing high heels, catch up. He moved over to her, whispered something in her ear that caused her to smile.

Suddenly I felt left out, and a trifle jealous.

11

I WAS GLAD TO BE BACK in the lounge chair, for it gave me a chance to take up where I had left off. Sitting next to me, the president gave the impression that he was entirely and exclusively at my disposal. Or perhaps that was my illusion, as it had been that of so many others.

It was time for the afternoon snack. The maître d' brought us a platter of fruit, which as protocol required he offered the president first. Mitterrand took the platter and offered it to me, then to the others, before setting it down on a table beside him. At which point he began devouring several fruits one after the other—an apple, a banana, whole bunches of grapes—as if he was using his teeth to fend off the ebbing of his life.

I've noted that people who are deathly ill often resort to this same tactic of eating voraciously, as if by gorging themselves they would keep death at bay.

"What book or books are you currently reading?" he asked, popping another grape in his mouth.

"None really," I answered a bit lamely. "And what about you?"

"De Tocqueville's *Memoirs*."

"You hadn't read them before?"

"No, and I might as well have saved myself the effort. They aren't really very good. They contain some interesting firsthand observations about the 1848 revolution, but de Tocqueville himself is not a very attractive person. He was such an arch-conservative."

The president popped three more grapes into his mouth, chewed and swallowed them, then went on. "I'm also reading Thomas Mann's *Joseph and His Brothers*. But my head is still filled with Saint Paul."

"Why is that?"

"I'm completely and passionately caught up by both his life and his work. He was one of the most prodigious figures in all human history. I have reconstructed his various travels, especially throughout Asia Minor. I'd love to retrace his footsteps myself, if I had the time."

"What did you learn from Saint Paul?"

"When he was young, he was of course an avowed enemy of the early Christians and actively persecuted them. And then, as we all know, he had his famous vision, or revelation, on the road to Damascus. And like all people who switch sides, he became overnight a militant Christian, a fanatic proselytizer, an outcast in his own way. At Antioch he founded his own community where, trying to establish a universal religion, he condemned among other things the rite of circumcision. On that score, he ran increasingly counter to the religious authorities of Jerusalem. He came very close to creating a schism. But then he finally decided to circumcise all his disciples personally, which he did. That was the Church's first major crisis, over a little bit of skin.

"When you think about it, the early Christians, led by James, were integrationists. They weren't for breaking away from the Jewish religion; they wanted to change it, make it more rigorous, more virtuous, more moral. They were forever standing in front of the Temple shouting themselves hoarse, bemoaning the many vices of the Hebrew religion. They made terrible pests of themselves, and every now and then the authorities would lose patience and stone one of them to death. What I like about Paul and his religious vision is its universality."

I remembered that it was Mitterrand who, twenty years before, if not more, had pressed upon me the necessity to read the Book of Ecclesiastes. One day, as we were traveling together by train, he pulled out a pocket edition of Ecclesiastes and began reading passages from it. As I remember it was the passage near the beginning: "All streams run to the sea."

When I asked him if Ecclesiastes was still his favorite bedside book, he looked at me with surprise and shook his head saying, "That's an exaggeration to say the least. There are so many books that pass across my night table I can't keep count. But Ecclesiastes is one I would qualify as a basic book, on the same level as Pascal's *Thoughts*. That's another mad book. What a shock it is when you suddenly come upon those pages in the Old Testament, written by God knows who, maybe Solomon himself, that are the magnificat of unbelief!"

I nodded, for I remembered having the same reaction when I had first read those same passages.

"Some of the best-known passages of our language come

from Ecclesiastes: 'Nothing new under the sun . . .'; 'All are from the dust, and all turn to dust again.' It's a veritable manual of skepticism. Not that I'm a great admirer of skepticism."

In his sheepfold at Latché a long time back I had noticed a well-thumbed Bible—also a pocket edition—looking for all the world like an overused phone book, lying not far from his bed.

Did he still enjoy dipping into the Bible?

"Constantly," he said. "But first you have to define which Bible you're referring to. I've never understood why they put the Old Testament, which is the book of God's justice, and the New Testament, which is the book of grace, between the same covers. They have nothing to do with each other."

"People talk about the violence of the Koran. But the violence of the Old Testament is striking to say the least, don't you agree?"

"Absolutely. I'm pleased to hear you say that."

He looked at me with gratitude, as if I'd just taken a great weight off his shoulders. I went on, " 'Thou shalt not kill,' admonishes the Old Testament, and yet that same Bible finds that stoning to death is a perfectly acceptable means of punishing someone."

"In the Bible there is blood on virtually every page."

"On a great many pages, in any case. It's only normal. According to the Bible, blood both purifies and sanctifies."

"And that's where all the wars, the massacres, all the looting and plundering emanate from," he said. "Have you ever noticed how frequently the Bible resounds with cries of death and destruction?"

"And when it isn't exhorting the faithful to avenge the Lord with all sorts of violence, it's calling for the immolation of animals. 'Without the shedding of blood there is no forgiveness of sins,' reads the Epistle to the Hebrews in the New Testament."

"And in the Old Testament it's not only animals that are being sacrificed. The law stipulates that Yahweh needs the sacrifice of young human flesh as well. 'Thou shalt give me the firstborn of your sons. Your firstborn shall remain for seven days with his mother, then on the eighth day thou shalt give him over to me.' Isn't that more or less how it goes?"

I wasn't sure, but said it sounded pretty accurate to me.

"After everything we've just said and quoted," he smiled, "are you still a Christian?"

"I guess you could say that I become one again each day of my life. What about you?"

He shrugged his shoulders, like a woodcutter after a hard day chopping down trees.

"One day you said to me that as you got older, nearer the end of your life, you *thought* you believed in God. Have you become a believer?" I asked.

"I've long defined myself as an agnostic, and that's still my position. It's not for lack of soul-searching, but the fact is I don't really know what I believe. Transcendence is a subject that fascinates me. But the matter of believing is something I've never been able to solve completely. Maybe I still might in the future."

And he laughed, but his laugh was more like a cough,

one of those terrible coughs that make you want to reach for your handkerchief.

"You have a religious temperament," I told him in his office at the Elysée months later. "So how can it be that you don't believe in God?"

"Let's just say I have a mystical soul and a rationalist brain and, like Montaigne, I am unable to choose between them. I don't know if I believe in God, but there are times when I am tempted to."

"What times are those?"

"Who doesn't need help and comfort from time to time, of the sort that the company of men can't provide? Those moments when suddenly you feel alone, lost in the immensity of the universe. Pascal said it better than I. There you are, your fragile body soon to be annihilated, and something within fills you with a belief in eternity. You have nothing else to turn to and the need is there."

That same day we had also talked about the question of faith and transcendence. He had made one further step along that road.

"Do you believe in the immortality of the soul?" I asked.

"Not especially. It would be rather embarrassing."

"Why then did you talk about the 'forces of the spirit' in one of your last speeches, when you said that you looked forward to listening to your successor's speech 'from wherever I may be at that time'?"

"I believe in the *power* of the spirit. Without it, what would man be after all?"

"But does the spirit have a life after death?"

"There's no way I can answer that question. After one's death, one's spirit remains the salt of the earth."

When I asked him again if by now he believed in God, he responded, "I still don't know. I must admit there are times when I'm *tempted* to believe, but the root of the term agnostic, the Greek *agnostos,* means 'unknown' or 'unknowable.' But I'm still an agnostic."

"Philosophically," I said, "are you still nowhere?"

"I've never posed the question in quite those terms. And being an agnostic is not being 'nowhere,' as you put it. That's taking a position."

"So in essence you're prepared to face death without God."

"Without knowing in my heart and mind that any ultimate reality does exist."

"You know Spinoza?"

"To some degree. I can't say I really know his work."

"I'm sure he's right in what he says, about the unity that exists between God, mind, and matter, as well as man's inability to understand his own actions. My problem is I find Spinoza very difficult to understand."

He gave a compassionate sigh. "Therein lies the problem," he said. "At a given moment in history philosophers stopped talking to the world and began talking only to themselves. In other words, they became unreadable. Just look at Plato by comparison: clear as a bell."

There was a moment's silence. The president shut his eyes

for a few seconds. When he opened them again, they were filled with mischief, and I was anticipating the worst.

"Do you still want to be a writer?" he asked.

"Let's say I'm still working on it."

"You've been working on it for a quarter of a century now. It's high time you chose another profession."

"Why?"

"Being a writer is boring and backbreaking. You should go into politics. You're made for it. You'd enjoy it, I promise you. There's still plenty of time. At your age, one can still switch professions." Saying which, he gave another deep sigh. "You're a very lucky man," he observed, though he failed to reveal the context of that observation.

"And I could say that you too have been a very lucky man," I retorted, thinking of his long career.

"But no longer. And if I have been lucky, I think it's safe to say that my past luck serves me no useful purpose now."

That day at Latché, alluding to earlier conversations we had had on the subject of death, I went back to the subject. "Do you still dream about immortality, of the notion of time stopping?" I asked.

"Oh, no!"

"To paraphrase Celine: Eternity must be very long, especially toward the end."

"Can you picture it? Being seventy-eight years old forever! The idea is unbearable. As it is, it's not easy."

"Does the fact that you've thought about death your entire life make it easier to confront today?"

"That perspective is so inscribed in everyone's life that it would be pretty abject to demean yourself when you know your time has come. I know that in a few days, a few months maybe, I'll be gone, but it's not the fact of dying that upsets me. It's the fact of no longer being alive." He paused, then, "Actually, you know, I feel I'm no longer of this world. What's more," and I could see a smile forming, "I have the feeling it's getting along just fine without me."

He said this with an air of nostalgia, as if he were indeed already only partly alive, already partly on the other side, and a certain degree of irony had crept into his words, like a veil, as he spoke of bygone years.

He had never believed much in anything. Now, I sensed, he no longer even believed in himself. He had once again become the young man of twenty-five who wrote to one of his early loves, his distant cousin Marie-Claire Sarrazin, whose nickname was "Clo," on September 28, 1942: "One should always keep in one's heart that divine reason that allows winter to light up the summer sun. Could I one day find satisfaction in the past, in the happiness of what has been? A difficult renunciation, one that forces us to ponder what we are doing here. The wisdom of the skeptics so closely resembles the despair that leaves within me a void that only eternity can satisfy."

12

"_My_ eyes are not what they used to be," he said, "but I'm still hoping I'll be able to go on reading till my dying day. My dream is to die with a book in my hand."

I understood how he felt. I'm terribly nearsighted myself. And I blame it on reading. When I was young I read incessantly, both in direct midday sunlight and in the deepest shadows. I read everywhere—in the back seat of the family car, during my math and physics courses, at the dinner table. I remember that I couldn't wait to leave the table after the evening meal so that I could run upstairs and slip in under the covers, where I would rejoin Dostoevsky, Steinbeck, Montaigne, Dickens, Flaubert, and a whole host of other writers too numerous to mention.

I spent my entire youth with a book in my hand.

The president had also spent most of his life with a book in his hand. As soon as he had a free moment, he would inevitably pull a novel or work of nonfiction from his pocket and disappear as long as he reasonably could, no matter what the circumstances. But he wasn't nearsighted. Unlike me, who wore glasses so thick they looked like magnifying glasses—until I switched to contact lenses—he had almost perfect eyesight. It was Mitterrand who introduced me to the work of Pierre Drieu la Rochelle.[1] "*Gilles* is you and me," he once said, as he loaned me a paperback copy of *Gilles* I'd noticed on one of his shelves. He also introduced me to the work of Chardonne.[2] At Latché that day, the thought crossed my mind that I might leave with a novel he'd slip in my pocket as I departed. But apparently he didn't feel like sharing any longer, not even a newly discovered literary love. He was beyond bone-weary, completely worn out.

"There are so many books still to read," he said.

"And to write."

"For you, not for me."

"The world is waiting for your memoirs."

"I won't ever write my memoirs, at least not in the classic sense of the term where you begin: 'I was born on October 26, 1916, at Jarnac, in the Charente department of France.' In other words, my autobiography. What I would like is to write five or six books focusing on the defining moments of my political career. But writing a book takes time, and I don't have much of that left."

He looked so bereft as he uttered those words that I should have reached over and covered his hand with mine. But I had neither the courage nor the audacity to make that simple gesture. I looked at his emaciated hand hanging there at his side, that hand that had not the right to an affectionate touch, and felt immensely sorry for it.

★

A few weeks later I had lunch with the president. His face was even more transparent than before. I was suffering for him, if one can ever truly suffer for another human being. I shouldn't have. He was in a positive, upbeat mood. He greeted me with a smile, which struck me as slightly mocking, and said, "Who is the greatest French writer of all time?"

"Is this a game?"

"If you can't think of an immediate answer, let me take a crack at it," he said. "As for myself, I'd pick Voltaire, although he wasn't an especially attractive human being. For instance, I hate the way he was always soliciting money from Frederick II, like a beggar. He also wrote a number of silly plays, which I have to admit enjoyed considerable success in their day. But he's a writer who fascinates me. Go back and reread *Candide*. It's amazingly fresh and as pertinent today as it was when it was written."

"And what about *Zadig*? Have you read *Zadig*?"

"Of course I have. And I also think Voltaire's correspondence is first rate."

"For some writers, their letters are among their best work. The invention of the telephone has been a crime against literature. Can you imagine what Flaubert would be without his correspondence?"

"You're quite right. When he wrote to his family and close friends he had so much more talent than when he wrote—I don't know—*Bouvard and Pécuchet*, for example."

"Or *Salammbo*, It's so incredibly old-fashioned it creaks."

"He worked too hard trying to get it right."

"That's why it's so obvious, so fabricated."

The president pretended to reflect for a moment then

added, "Not all that long ago I think I would have given the title of 'Best French Writer' to Chateaubriand. I love the way he wrote. And his portraits of people are quite extraordinary."

"His portrait of Talleyrand, of course."

"But also of Charles X."

"Chateaubriand would have been sublime if only he'd been able to rise above himself. He seemed completely incapable of introspection."

"It's true," he agreed, "that he was vain to a fault, almost to the point of ridicule."

"Like all people writing their autobiographies, he always had to put himself center stage. 'It was I who did this or that, I who saw this or that, I who thought this or that.' "

The president shook his head. "It's a dangerous undertaking, writing one's memoirs," he said. "But when you succeed, as Chateaubriand did, the results can be spectacular. The rest of his work is mediocre. *The Genius of Christianity* and *Atala* are both worthless in my view."

"But his pages on Napoleon place him in the first ranks of French literature," I asserted.

"He really did put Napoleon in his rightful place," the president said. "But nonetheless he didn't manage to kill the legend. Once legends take root, there's no way you can really kill them." He paused, then came back to the subject of autobiographical writing. "Writing one's memoirs is always difficult," he said, "and sometimes very cruel, self-revealing. Do you remember that passage in Jules Renard's *Journal* [3] where he and Octave Mirbeau [4] are talking in the family garden when they hear the sound of splashing water coming from the direction of the well. They go over to see what's causing it and discover that Jules' mother has fallen into the well. And what does he say in his *Journal* about the incident? 'What a strange way to turn me into an orphan.' Not one iota of concern for his mother. It's all about me, me, me. How tough can you get!"

"Being tough is a literary artifice. I'm sure that in real life he was a pussy cat."

"Nothing I've ever read by or about him would make me believe that."

"To think that a good third of Renard's journal ended up in his wife's stove, under the pretense that it was either too spiteful or too indiscreet. To make matter's worse, it was done with the knowledge and consent of Renard's publisher."

"There are so many masterpieces that remain unknown or undiscovered. Assuming they too haven't already gone up in smoke."

"Four billion years from now, when the sun burns out, I think it's safe to say there will be a certain leveling effect. No further room for disagreement."

He gave a deep sigh, gazing up at the ceiling, as if searching for the sun. "Meanwhile, the sun is still up there in fine fettle," he said. "Which is more than you can say for me."

There was a moment of embarrassment, on his part doubtless because he regretted giving way, even momentarily, to self-pity, and on mine because I simply didn't know what to say in response.

"If you had to sum up your autobiography, what would you say?"

"I wouldn't even try," he said. "But if forced, maybe the best way I could describe what I'd like it to have been would be to say, Voltaire writing *The Social Contract*. Rousseau[5] tried, but he really botched it up completely, didn't he?"

"But still, you like Rousseau's ideas, don't you?"

"Because they were strong opinions. But I really don't like the man."

"You know the old chestnut: 'If you had to choose between Voltaire and Rousseau, who would you pick? The answer is: Diderot.' Is that how you feel, too?"

"Diderot was a great writer, but I'd still choose Voltaire, who I think incarnates better than anyone else the spirit of the French."

"You are, as Victor Hugo might have phrased it, a man whose mind is always somewhere else. Whenever you've dreamed of being someone else, who did you envision being? A writer?"

"I would have liked to be a writer, yes. But the response has already been given. I was in love with the world of action."

"Any regrets? I mean about not becoming a writer, or of your opting for politics?"

"None."

"Not a moment of doubt or dissatisfaction?"

"When you're involved in the real world, you dream of a life of meditation. But after three months of meditating in the desert, you inevitably say to yourself, I'd really like to *do* something. So you start dreaming and hoping that a camel might happen by so that you can climb up and get yourself back to the world of action."

And once you're on the camel, there's no use trying to seek refuge behind the saddle.

The president got to his feet. "What do you say we go inside. It's getting a bit nippy, don't you agree?"

I didn't agree. And I suspected that he didn't think so either, but I had neither the desire nor courage to contradict him. Besides, it was coming up to dusk. So I followed the president, who was wending his way toward the sheepfold, followed by Anne Lauvergeon and Jacques Pilhan. Once there, we all took seats on the leather easy chairs that graced the presidential bedroom.

"I often come down here alone," he observed. "Since I don't have a kitchen, I usually have lunch in a local restaurant. Since I've been ill, they bring me breakfast in bed. Being ill does have its virtues, you know; people are much more solicitous than they ever were." He frowned, then went on, "I know more than I care to know about prostate cancer. We have a long history of prostate cancer in my family. My father died of it. My brother Philippe died of it after only a brief illness. And my oldest brother Robert also contracted it six years ago. He fought it tooth and nail and won. I'm still on the fence, so to speak. The question is, which way will I fall?"

The fact was, he had already fallen. But he was pretending that he didn't realize it.

13

*T*HE PRESIDENT WAS SILENT, which I suspected was due to his innate reserve or, more likely, to his thinking about those close to him who had passed away. Suddenly he broke the silence. "Poor Mother," was all he said. I didn't comment, for I was expecting him to carry that comment further. But he did not.

Night approached, slowly enveloping us. For him, it brought with it thoughts of gloom and doom. When he remained silent, the president's mouth became that of a dying man, his lips slightly ajar, just wide enough for infinity to slip in.

Suddenly he stood up. "Come over here," he said, "I want to show you something," and he headed toward a bookshelf on which stood a picture of his mother. The expression on her face was a mixture of sadness and resignation. "She died so young," he murmured.

He pointed to a watercolor painting, quite well done though hardly inventive, the blues of which were too heavy, revealing the work to be that of a novice.

"My mother painted that," he said proudly. "Not bad, eh?"

Then he picked up a photograph of both his parents. She was a stout woman, massive really, and she was ripe for motherhood. You could tell she was filled with high principles. It was from her that he had inherited his stubbornness, the quality that enabled him to move heaven and earth to gain his desired ends.

His father was decked out in his Sunday best, looking for all the world like a martinet, brimming with dreams of grandeur, a ladies' man beset with problems of conscience. It was as plain as the nose on his face: he was a man who firmly believed he was the center of the universe, a trait he had passed on to his son, François. I noted that the president spent far less time looking at his father than he did at his mother.

After having studied the array of photographs on the library shelves, we all sat down on the presidential bed, a bed so simple that it belied that title, the bed to which he repaired so often for his vacations and weekends. It was poorly made up, with a plain white coverlet, the bed linen rumpled, fit perhaps for a monk or a soldier but certainly not for a Don Juan. Scattered around the bed was a disorderly assortment of belongings that would have sufficed to withstand a prolonged siege: a bottle of mineral water, an apple, a banana, a huge clutter of medicines, piles and piles of books, among which I noticed de Tocqueville's *Memoirs,* Thomas Mann's *Joseph and His Brothers,* the Jerusalem Bible, a book on the Charente region of France, another on the Drôme.

The clutter reminded me of my mother's bed after it had become clear she had lost her bout with cancer.

We all looked at a whole parade of other photographs

that the president kept passing around, mostly of people we didn't know. Members of his family for the most part, both immediate and distant. When I recognized in one of the photos his daughter Mazarine, who had been born out of wedlock, I quickly moved to the next picture, pretending I hadn't seen her. He appeared not to see her either. But I suspect that for some time now he had decided to no longer see.

For a long time the president had practiced what Baudelaire referred to as "the art of double conscience." From the window, he would watch himself walking down the street, then climbing the stairs, opening the door, making love, then leaving to go make a speech somewhere. That was his strength.

One day several weeks after my trip to Latché, he said to me, "You have a sense of perspective. That's important. Something one should always have and keep. You should always look down on yourself from above, as if you were watching yourself from an upstairs window. That makes you grow up. In my case, I grew up too much. Which is why I'm going to die." Saying which, he smiled, as if pleased by his turn of phrase. The distance he took between his real self and his public persona was also a kind of indifference. As death drew nearer, that indifference had become staggering. Nothing any longer moved him, or even seemed to make any impression on him. That day I remember hearing him talk about the "Mazarine affair" with a mixture of sangfroid and fatalism that I had never seen before when the subject mattered to him personally.

When in November 1994 the weekly magazine *Paris-*

Match had revealed the existence of his illegitimate daughter Mazarine, with photos to prove it, he had said to me, "Frankly, that whole story isn't a tragedy. Not even a drama. Everybody who mattered to me already knew about it. My wife knew about Mazarine. If the child had been a baby when it came out, that could have proved embarrassing for all concerned. But for a nineteen-year-old girl . . . please!"

"She was born before 1981. So I guess you could claim the whole story falls under the statute of limitations," I joked.

"Legally you're right of course. But if the story had broken even last year it would have been extremely difficult for my daughter. She hadn't yet taken her examination to get into l'Ecole Normale.[1] A year ago she was far less self-assured than she is today. I think she's now in excellent shape. When the story became public, she wasn't overly upset. She's really quite a remarkable young lady, Mazarine. Extremely talented, with a strong philosophical bent. She wants to write, you know. I don't know what she'll end up doing, but I can assure you she's going to become someone."

For a moment, his eyes shone with paternal pride. A predator's smile. "I have sinned a lot," he said, then, qualifying, he added, "in my personal life, that is. I've sinned and sinned again. Endlessly. My only 'punishment' has been Mazarine. I've been a lucky man." He laughed, his laugh welling from the tomb in which he already pictured himself. "I've been accused of every possible sin," he went on. "I've been accused of being a liar, an ex-fascist, a former collaborator, a kapo in the death camps during the war, someone who has peopled the world with his illegitimate offspring. People have discovered my bastards in virtually every corner of France, you know.

Oh, yes, not to mention one in Sweden. It would seem that I've also been accused of having ordered the assassination of a whole host of people. Murders that I then covered up by claiming they were suicides. And gotten off scot-free. A real latter-day Landru, with the difference that I got away with my crimes. The best way to respond is to laugh. But unlike de Gaulle, who sued those who he claimed defamed him, I prefer to ignore them. I can tell you, though, a great number of people profited greatly from having related all this non-sense about me to the scandal sheets, or to whoever cared to listen."

I decided to raise the level of the conversation and bring up the question of freedom of the press. "On the basis of a people's right to know, the press has itself in recent years thrown off any kind of self-restraint and printed all manner of embarrassing stories about people in government. Do you see this as posing any kind of danger for democracy?"

"No. In the long run, people will get tired of these un-restrained powers, which nonetheless do raise the question whether democracy can or should endure."

"Do you view the media, and the judiciary, as 'unre-strained powers'?"

"I think the French judicial system is in pretty good shape, even if there are those who would like to give judges greater power. As for the media, I see it as a proliferation that feeds on itself and is running rampant."

"So you do believe the media has too much power?"

"I wouldn't be so concerned about its having too much power if there were some rules and regulations it had to abide by."

"In most countries of the world today, the media has become so invasive it thinks nothing of moving right into people's bedrooms. Do you find it normal that it lays bare every aspect of people's personal lives?"

"I couldn't care less. But on the other hand, journalists who do so should themselves be prepared to pay the piper as well."

"To bring the question closer to home: what was your reaction when you learned that *Paris-Match* was going to run the story about Mazarine?"

"Obviously, I was not exactly overjoyed. But it was not as if I wasn't expecting it. And besides," he added, "I was quite flattered to be shown in the company of such a charming young woman."

"She is extremely pretty, isn't she?"

His show of surprise at my question was too marked to be sincere. "Really? Do you think so? It's true, people do find her very attractive."

"What did you learn from that whole experience?"

"That the French are much more sophisticated than I had imagined. They seemed to take the whole thing very much in stride. Even approve. Strange, no?"

"I suspect that they probably approved of the fact that you didn't try to deny it."

"A pity I don't have a few more revelations up my sleeve."

"Who says you don't?"

"I say. On that point I can assure you. There will be no further surprises. If I had any others out there, I would have owned up to them as well." A mixture of silence and inner reflection. Then, "One thing is sure. No one is going to send me a telegram like the one that François Mauriac, the arch-Catholic, is said to have received from the atheist André Gide after Gide died. The telegram read:

> DEAR FRANÇOIS: IT TURNS OUT
> THERE'S NO HELL. GO OUT AND SIN TO
> YOUR HEART'S CONTENT. PLEASE PASS
> THE WORD TO CLAUDEL.[2]
> (SIGNED) ANDRÉ GIDE."

He loved women. A real Don Juan. In their presence, his tendency was to say, Thank you, yes, I'd like them all. That was why he took such pains not to belong to any of them.

Few could resists his advances. Like an expert fisherman, he reeled them in slowly, using as bait a combination of consummate tact, an enticing smile, fluttering eyelids, and gentle words of love. Patient to a fault, without regard for the time it might take, he charmed them one and all, enveloped them in charm, with all the seduction of a courtly abbot, until they finally succumbed.

Apparently, from all reports, he was a true predator. At least twice or three times, when he had asked me to meet him at eight in the morning at his apartment on the rue de Bièvre in Paris, I would see him arrive looking for all the world like a conspirator, exhausted and unshaven. He resembled not so much a night owl as a wolf that had been out on the prowl till dawn. A conspiratorial smile or wink sufficed to let me know what he'd been up to.

And yet he was really quite sentimental. There were

many among his conquests to whom he promised the moon, claiming that he was ready to throw everything over and begin life anew with them. Not only in Europe, but in the States as well. Somewhere in the heart of Texas. Or deep in the deserts of Arizona. The women with whom he was in love were the only beings on the face of the earth capable of making him abandon his cynicism. He adored it when he felt they loved him. He could not help being swept up in the heat of passion, even when his ailing body was not up to the task at hand. Every day he had to call his ex-lovers, his current lovers, and of course those he was still hoping to seduce. When he broke off an affair, he always left the door open to a possible reconciliation.

Some evenings, when the president gave way to a mixture of desire and nostalgia, he pretended to be Casanova, whose *Memoirs* he treasured. "Somewhere in his *Memoirs*," he said, "Casanova talks about a man who has just been thrown over by the woman he loves, and he's beside himself with grief. Then a pretty woman happens by who catches his eye. As if by magic, he's completely cured."

Mitterrand had never been bowed down with grief over a lost love. He always landed on his feet.

"What's the most beautiful love word you know?" I asked.

Without a moment's hesitation he said: "Yes." And with that he began to quote by heart the final lines of James Joyce's *Ulysses*, where Molly Bloom finally yields to her ardent admirer, one of the loveliest and most affirmative passages in literature: "And yes I said yes I will yes."

He had a foot fetish. He'd been known to ask his

conquests to take off their shoes in his presence. After which, he would tenderly caress the lady's ankle, her heel, the sole of her foot. It was his way of getting acquainted.

On the other hand, he was always reluctant to bare his own feet. His toenails were excessively long. "I just can't bring myself to trim them," he said to me one day. "It's as if I were cutting off part of myself."

I was sure that Mazarine would never sit on this white coverlet in the sheepfold at Latché. Because he had so compartmentalized his personal life, and put each of his family or friends in a separate drawer, he could never remember who he had put where. And he had become so enmeshed in his own lies that he no longer knew where the truth lay. That was why he seemed so alone.

"This illness is insidious," he said. "The problem is, the doctors tend to give up too quickly. Which is why I give them such hell."

He had lost everything, except for his morale, which surfaced every now and then and buoyed his spirits, at least temporarily.

One day the president asked me to join him for a walk. What I didn't know when he invited me was that he planned to take our walk in a cemetery. I met him at the Passy Cemetery, near Trocadero in Paris. A lovely cemetery, completely sheltered from the wind by the high walls that surround it on all sides. Death must be peaceful and gentle here under the yews.

People of substance like their lives to be peaceful, even after they die. Walking among these handsome tombs, one can understand why people want to pass on to their reward. It's such a beautiful spot you'd think you were in a painting, a cross between a Corot and a Sisley.

The problem with death is, you're obliged to leave. But afterward, in the Passy Cemetery, all is silence, flowers, trees, and happiness. You spend your death in the country. This said, one has to consider that, in so bucolic a setting, people may be bored to tears.

"It's worth the trip, don't you agree?" he said as we strolled the walkways between the graves. "Actually, I prefer cemeteries to museums. Strange as it may sound, I find them much livelier."

That day his intention was to visit the tomb of Marie Bashkirtseff, which sat on a rise just to the right as you entered the cemetery. A mausoleum erected to her glory, part bourgeois salon, part artist's studio. The president descended into the crypt and knelt before her tomb, which was of white marble. Its only inscription was her name and the dates of her birth and death: 1860–1884.

Bashkirtseff was a Russian, who in her brief life had been a painter, a sculptor, and a writer; a fervent Christian, and an out-and-out adventuress. Like us all, she was a child whose head was filled with dreams. But one by one her dreams crumbled: love, marriage, glory, and finally life itself, as she was carried off at the age of twenty-four by galloping consumption. She died during the night of October 30, 1884, and her last words were: "We'll all end up together."

Together, but with whom? Perhaps with her English

duke, or maybe with her Bonapartist nobleman, on both of whom she had lavished such love and adoration that they had bolted, leaving her bereft. But it wasn't her fault. She simply was possessed of an excess of love. For everyone. In her last will and testament she wrote, among other things: "What I ardently desire is that the poor be helped and sheltered as much as possible during the cold months of winter."

When she breathed her last there was no one at her side, no masculine hand to hold hers. Men only came into her life in a meaningful way after she had left this world. When the funeral procession headed off in the direction of the Russian Orthodox church in the rue Daru, the whole world suddenly fell in love with her. Even the normally unflappable Maurice Barrès[3] joined in the general delirium: "Marie Bashkirtseff," he enthused, "incarnated in her lovely self at least five or six exceptional souls."

Above all, she was a woman who loved to talk about love. "There's something truly beautiful," she wrote on November 5, 1878, when she was eighteen, "something old-fashioned about love: the abasement of a woman before the superiority of the man she loves has to be the greatest demonstration of pride and self-respect that a superior woman can ever make." She was a young woman possessed, who dared to write what most of us don't even dare think. On June 13, 1876, when she was only sixteen, she penned this: "God did not make me the way I am for no purpose; He cannot have instilled in me the power to see everything with such utter clarity in order to torment me by offering nothing in return. Such a supposition contradicts the very nature of God, who is a being of kindness and mercy. Either I shall be fulfilled or I shall die. So be it." And exactly a month later she wrote: "Good God! Grant me the life I desire or let me die!"

"Does Marie still excite you, even now, more than a century after her death?" I asked with, I am sure, a note of concern.

"It's strange," he said, "but I think that's the right word: she excites me. First of all because she was, so far as anyone knew, the very model of chastity. One might have thought that she was the creation of Bernardin de Saint-Pierre. Now that we've discovered that her diary was heavily censored, what attracts me about her is the fact she was a completely free spirit, one of those rare creatures who was not afraid to reveal the deepest secrets of her heart. In fact, she was 'Belle du Seigneur.' "

"She was a woman in a hurry," I said, "who wanted to mix love and ambition. Frankly, I don't think she's your type."

"Maybe, but I'm fascinated by that very facet of her makeup—she wanted it all and she wanted it soon. And I also love her exuberance in all things. Like all people who sense their lives will be short, Marie knew she couldn't wait. She didn't simply devour life; she gulped it down as fast as she could."

"If you had met her, would you have fallen for her?"

"Maybe. But you know, women like that don't really have the capacity to love. They only pass by; they never stay put. They feel they always have to move on, because they're afraid of death."

He said that with a glimmer of disdain, as if he, unlike

Marie or her ilk, was not afraid of death. But it was a false glimmer.

That same day, with his hand pressed hard against his hip as if he was trying to ease the pain welling from somewhere deep within, the president said to me, and I remember the words exactly, "The terrible thing about cancer is that in the long run it takes away your zest for life. Once in a while I get it back, but not very often. But when it does return, it makes me so happy that I keep saying over and over, 'How lucky I am to be living a day as wonderful as this!' "

"Does that happen often?"

"Often enough. Take this last November 11, my final Armistice Day as president of France. How I loved that whole ceremony! I looked out over the horizon, and I felt better, I assure you. I said to myself, A page of history has been turned. I thought: it's all over. And I felt the better for it. As you see, I'm still enjoying life, at least some of its better moments."

He smiled, but the smile quickly turned into a grimace of pain.

"The days go by so quickly," he said.

"As do the years, the decades."

"And not even time to look back at the past."

"It's a mistake not to look back."

"One I have committed, like everyone else. The day we come into the world, we start the process that will lead to our own destruction. And yet we go on believing that life will last forever. Believe me, that's something I believe less and less."

"You shouldn't talk that way, Mr. President."

"I'm still lucid, that's all I can say. At times I realize how horribly painful it is simply to remain standing. For example, the last Anglo-French summit meeting at Chartres was sheer torture for me: an hour without being able to sit down is rough in my condition. But I managed. I've held out against all sorts of odds in my life. I don't see why I can't hold out against this illness."

He uttered these words in so fluty a voice that one sensed he didn't really believe what he was saying.

The president had always had a weakness for fortune-tellers and clairvoyants. He could listen to them for hours telling him about himself. One day in the fall some years back, after he had finished lunch, an extraordinary, super-lucid character was brought to him: Aum Farouk, known as Hadjehe, a fat Arab woman who was so round she seemed to roll in rather than walk. She squatted down on the floor and asked for a pot full of water, which I went to fetch. She dipped her hands into the water as she murmured some prayers.

I started to leave the room, but the president signaled me to remain.

"Please stay," he said, "I have no secrets, even from you."

"This morning," Hadjehe said after a long pause, "you had a blood test."

"Yes, you're right," Mitterrand said, taken aback.

"You're afraid."

"True."

"All you think about is your illness."

"True."

"You're wracked with pain throughout your entire body: your back, your legs, your chest, everywhere."

"Yes, that's so."

She bowed again over the pot of water, as if looking into the future there, then asked to see the presidential foot. Mitterrand obliged by pulling up one trouser leg.

What she said then was not translated for him. Later I learned what it was: "I cannot see anything. This man has neither past nor future. Nothing. He's going to die. It's not a matter of months, but of weeks."

The president's face suddenly darkened, as if he had understood her words. He already knew. His haggard eyes revealed what he was thinking.

There was nothing he could do. He looked like all those patients suffering from terminal cancer when it's too late and they seem to be looking at you from beyond the grave, from some point in eternity. They were the same eyes my mother had on her deathbed. Eyes that begged for help, knowing that help would never come.

Death would be so simple if you didn't have to die.

Every man who comes into this world is put here for a purpose. Often the goal is simply to find the woman he loves; others aim at nothing more than material success. But sometimes, far more rarely, it happens that a man believes his role in life is to change the world or to visit upon the earth the ravages of war, which gives him, momentarily, the feeling that he is superior, a great man in the midst of lesser creatures, until death moves in and reduces him to dust, as it does to all creatures.

I have often asked myself what François Mitterrand was seeking here below, knowing how strongly he felt about the futility and inanity of earthly strivings. Certainly he was not seeking glory. He knew how fleeting it was. The problem with men in general, and world leaders in particular, is that they feel they are immortal, whereas in truth posterity usually lasts for no more than several decades, sometimes a few centuries, or, in very rare cases, two or three millennia. In terms of the cosmos, or of our own ordinary sun, posterity is meaningless.

The president had not come into this world to wreak havoc on his country, as some others had, notably Napoleon. Chateaubriand once wrote that Napoleon was dragging in his wake the doors of Janus, behind which he had piled up a mountain of corpses to make sure the doors could not be opened again.[4]

In Mitterrand's case, these corpses were not human. The mountains he had used as barricades were the mountains of lost illusions, illusions in which he had once believed and no longer did, which had the stink of the catacombs about them.

Not that he had harbored any of his illusions for very long. Now that the shadow of death was moving closer and he was preparing his own sepulcher, he made no bones about the fact that he preferred his own company to that of the ideologues that this frightful century had successively laid to rest. He advanced without so much as looking at others, following his ego and his destiny. He saw—or hoped to find—his future in eternity. One day I heard him say: "If I had the choice, I'd like to die in some absolutely beautiful place. Aswan,[5] for instance, where you feel so important it's as if the sky belongs to you or you are part of the sky. When you open the windows of the Old Cataract Hotel in the morning, you feel as if you are one with the universe, the day after the creation of the world. Or in Venice, where you feel so small, so insignificant, that you already feel engulfed by eternity." And then he said later, "I'd really like to be interred in the Pantheon. That's where my presidency began. It seems to me only good and proper that that's where it should end. But the Socialists will see to it that doesn't happen."

With one foot in the grave, or as he waited for death to decide when to move in, that was the tone and tenor of his thoughts about the afterlife.

It was fast coming up to dusk. I could see that the president dreaded the darkness that was moving in, obliterating everything in its wake. He was afraid.

To help get him through the night he needed a helping hand, a feminine hand. Or a good book. I felt that he was truly sorry to see us leave.

Anne Lauvergeon placed an open manila folder on his lap. The president began signing a number of letters, mechanically, as if he were not paying attention to what he was signing, when suddenly he stopped and exclaimed, "Oh, no! I can't believe it. How can anyone make such a mistake? I *hate* spelling mistakes!"

Then he glanced at the press clippings she had brought.

He paused over one editorial, which he quickly scanned before tossing it aside. "Stupidities," he muttered. "They're all so dumb. I can't believe people would waste their time on such inanities."

Then he closed the folder, with a gesture that was more one of weariness than anger, and looked me straight in the eyes for what seemed like a long time.

I was completely taken in by the candor I read there. As life was receding from him, he reached out increasingly to others. For the moment, he was reduced to nothing more than one glance in search of another. I offered him mine. We were locked together, somewhere far from the world.

"We've got to go," Jacques Pilhan said with a certain urgency, "otherwise we'll miss the plane."

The president walked with us to the car. He bid us each good-bye, in his usual laconic manner. But when the car reached the end of the driveway, I turned around and saw through the back window that the president was still standing there, waving. His gesture, and that image, reminded me of my American grandmother, during the last months of her life. The juxtaposition of those two images—my grandmother and the president—made me think: he hasn't long now.

The pine trees of Latché were merging into the darkening sky. I felt I was in mourning, as I always did when I saw death hounding someone relentlessly. It wasn't that I pitied him, but I was sorry that he, like Louis XIV, like almost all of the kings of France, was making no effort to shield from the world the visible ravages of approaching death.

14

*F*OUR MONTHS LATER, despite all my concerns and the dire predictions of most political pundits, the president was still alive. Not well, but alive. The transparency I had noted earlier was even more pronounced. "It's the chemotherapy that makes me translucent," he commented ironically. But I noted that he had regained his old smile.

It was the first day of the New Year. The pine trees at Latché were stirred by a wind that was slight but carried an undeniable midwinter bite. When it caught you unawares it suddenly chilled you to the bone. Latché seemed motionless beneath the winter sky. Add a touch of frost and you would have thought you were in a Monet still life.

Inside the house was warm, but the president seemed as stiff as the trees outside. He was a mere shadow of his former self—except for the smile—and it was all he could do to move from one easy chair to another. But like all deathly ill people locked in their metaphysical fortresses, he was counting on the cavalry to gallop forth and save him at the last second.

As we sat down for lunch, he deployed a veritable army of pills in front of his plate. "These are my troops," he explained. "I'm at war." As if to explain the nature of the war, he pointed to his lower abdomen. "You can't imagine the titanic struggle taking place in there," he said. "Sniper fire from every angle, which explains why I'm so tired. The cancer snipers never let up, not for a single minute. They're giving me no quarter. When it's over, one of us will be dead: either me or the cancer. It will be either my Austerlitz or my Waterloo."[1]

He laughed. In fact, he was in fine fettle that day. I had the distinct feeling that he was hoping I would humor him with the latest supply of jokes and humorous gossip, but for the life of me I couldn't think of anything new. My problem is, I forget jokes the minute I hear them, so I have to fall back on the few I carry as permanent baggage. Like the one about Queen Victoria. When her long reign was at last coming to an end at the beginning of the twentieth century, her son Edward, before he assumed the crown, asked her if she had any important advice to give him. "Only this," she had said. "Make sure you go to the bathroom before you attend any royal functions." But I knew he had heard it before, probably more than once, so I decided to spare him not only that one but my meager store of other stories as well.

When he realized I was going to fail him, he decided to tell one of his own. Not a joke, but a grotesque tale he had experienced himself, which I had never heard before, about a girl from his hometown he generously referred to only as Jeanne F.

"When I was young," he said, "Jeanne F. lived not far from us in Jarnac, on the rue Porte-Coton. She was very poor and to boot she was extremely ugly. And very fat, so I really pitied her. Years later, when I was mayor of Château-Chinon, she suddenly appeared and asked to see me.

"She had changed. First of all, she was even fatter than before. She had also dyed her hair, which contrasted starkly with the ruddiness of her face. What was more, she was wearing a scraggly, long-haired fur coat, the kind of coat that women who are trying to emulate rich ladies wear.

"As soon as she entered my office, she threw herself in my arms—almost suffocating me—and said, 'I need your help.' I asked her what I might do to help. 'I'll tell you,' she said. 'After my mother died, I learned that I was the heiress of a fortune left by an elderly American couple whose name was Mallet.' 'That's great,' I said. 'Congratulations.' 'But wait,' she went on, 'that's not all. The Americans left their money not only to me but to *all* their direct descendants who live in the Nièvre department of France.' 'I'm still not sure what you want from me,' I said. 'I need you to compile a list of all the people named Mallet who live in the region,' she replied. 'I've set up an association called the Mallet Clan. The inheritance doesn't kick in until we find all the descendants.' 'I don't think it's within my jurisdiction to do that,' I countered. Her face clouded over visibly. 'Careful,' she said a trifle menacingly. 'The Mallets are all voters. And there a lot of Mallets in your election district. I already control a good portion of them through my association. I've raised money and have a Mallet Clan office.'

"In short, by the time she left my office there was a distinct chill in the air, although in the course of her visit she had managed at one point to touch me when she evoked the memory of my mother. 'What a wonderful woman your mother was,' she had murmured, with obvious sincerity.

"Some time later I ran into her by chance again. She

was even fatter than before, and her face was even redder. Also, I could have sworn that the strands of fur on her coat were longer than ever. Anyway, she informed me that she had started a new association, this one for women who had been betrayed by their husbands. 'And I would suspect it will do very well,' I ventured. 'It will,' she assured me. 'There's a definite need in the market there. We have all sorts of professionals backing us: doctors, professors, priests. And we've bought ourselves an island.'

"That was the last I heard of her for some time. Then, several months later, I ran into her again. Fatter than ever. Redder than ever. The fur of her coat seemed even longer than before. She informed me that she had just founded another association, this one for husbands whose wives had cheated on them. 'There are a lot more cuckolds in this world than you'd imagine,' she announced proudly, puffing out her already voluminous chest. 'This new association is doing fantastically well. We've even bought another island.' I offered her my hearty congratulations, but she was already going on. 'I had the idea,' she said, 'of getting the two associations to spend weekends together, don't you see. They have a lot in common.' 'I'm sure they do,' I agreed. 'I bet these ladies and gentlemen can swap all kinds of stories that will keep them occupied through the cold winter nights.'

"Then I didn't see her again for several years. One day I was standing on the station platform at Nevers waiting for my local train when the window of a the chic Train Bleu on its way to Italy, on a platform across the way, was suddenly lowered and who stuck her head out but Jeanne F. 'Come over here,' she ordered, 'I want to introduce you to my husband, Prince Ayubi.' I did as she bid, and when I entered her first-class compartment, she pointed to a poor devil sprawled out on the seat and wrapped from head to toe in garments that resembled blankets, looking more like a North African beggar than a prince. So Jeanne F. had indeed become Princess Ayubi, and before long one began to see her picture in the weekly magazines and scandal sheets that feed on the rich and famous, next to the aristocrats, the deposed royals, the movie stars, and God knows who else.

"And then one day I opened the paper to find that Princess Ayubi had been arrested. Her crime was to have set up all sorts of phony associations that had been milking poor innocent victims of their life savings. She was found guilty and sentenced to prison. Being a softy, I sent her several food parcels while she was in jail.

"Some time later I was attending a rally of a new political group I had started. It was just getting off the ground, and there were no more than a hundred delegates in attendance. Suddenly, as I walking past the group from my home department whom should I see but Jeanne F. 'I'm your delegate from Nièvre,' she announced proudly. I asked her what she was up to now and she said that she had just formed a company selling plots of land on the moon. 'Really,' I said, trying not to sound surprised. 'And how is it doing?' 'We've already sold four,' she said."

The president's guffaw was, I presumed, the signal that his story about Jeanne F. was over. Or perhaps that he was about to tell another, which proved to be the case. This was about a curious legal case he had been involved in when he had been a government minister in the 1950s. There was a little town in the Nièvre, called Gouloux, that had been having a problem with a local wolf. It seems the wolf had been preying on the village sheep. The elected officials of Gouloux, under pressure to do something, asked the villagers to take down their hunting rifles and go out and kill the culprit. And indeed their efforts were crowned with a kill, but not the one they had planned. One of the hunters, on his way home, was making his way through a barbed wire enclosure when his gun accidentally went off, killing a fellow hunter. There was a trial. The wife of the victim sued the hunter. The surviving hunter in turn sued the village officials who had mobilized him to kill the wolf.

"The judge found for the clumsy hunter: the village of Gouloux was fined 50,000 francs—an enormous sum at the time—and ordered to pay said sum to the grieving widow. The problem was, the village was up in arms at what it considered a terrible miscarriage of justice, for the simple reason that sometime between the shooting and the award of money the grieving widow had taken up with the hunter who had killed her husband. Feelings were running so high at Gouloux that I made a decision: the state should shoulder that financial burden. The only problem was, how should I categorize the expense? I finally decided to put it in the column under 'Agricultural Disasters.' "

The president glanced over at me. He was clearly exhausted, but pleased at having told the two stories, both of which I had found charming, for they had taken him mercifully back to earlier times and places where life had been simple.

"Why don't you write all that down?" I suggested.

"You can have them," he said. "I offer them to you."

I had drunk more wine at lunch than I should have, and I knew that I would never be able to remember them accurately. So I excused myself for a moment and slipped into the bathroom, where I jotted down a few notes to jog my memory later on.

Later, we went down to join the whole family clan, which had been lunching in a nearby restaurant. The family members had obviously been commiserating with one another about the president's declining health, for they all looked like mourners when we entered the restaurant and ordered coffee. But the president was not dead; far from it, he dominated the conversation from then on, regaling everyone with other stories.

Then, suddenly, I saw something freeze in his eyes. A bolt of pain had just hit and refused to pass. It was as if he had left his body. Little by little his face was transformed into a death mask. He was no longer with us.

He asked if I would accompany him back home. As we neared the little staircase leading up into the Latché garden, he seized my arm. "Do you mind giving me a hand?" I felt his fingernails, which were long, digging into my flesh. He was clinging to me as he was clinging to everything: to life, to power, to pleasure. But our ascent up the stairs was easy, for I realized he weighed virtually nothing any more. He was as light as the icy air borne in by the raging sea.

That day again, when he said good-bye, it was with a tenderness I had rarely heard, and I had the distinct feeling it was a final farewell. He finished with a gentle tap on my shoulder, and his look was so piercing that it remained with me not only throughout the ride home but for days thereafter.

Yet we saw each other again a number of times. But then it was as if he were already in another realm, a place somewhere between life and death. His already transparent body had become strange, almost unhuman.

One day the rumor of his death raced through Paris. I put in a call to Latché and it was he who immediately answered the phone.

"You sound good," I said.

"How can you tell?" he asked

"Your voice."

"One's voice is a reflection," he laughed. "It can't ever hide anything. The fact is, I feel fine today." A pause. "I'm here in my sheepfold, sitting in an easy chair looking out the window. Each leaf is a mirror in which the sky is reflected. My dogs are lying at my feet. In a few minutes I'm going to get up, go over to my desk, and write down what I'm thinking at this moment. Who could ask for anything more? I think I'm happy. I only regret that the cancer has apparently metastasized. Throughout my body, I'm told."

Somehow he found the strength—or courage—to laugh. After which we spent several minutes chattering about anything and everything.

He also called me several times over the next few weeks for no apparent reason. He wanted to know what was up, what the latest news was. He ended with, "Let's have lunch."

"Shall we set a date?"

"No. I'll call you later. We'll set a date then."

The reason he didn't want to fix a date too far in advance was that he could never be sure how he'd be feeling. Often he'd call less than half an hour before the appointed hour. Above all, he wanted to keep up appearances. And almost without exception he managed to put up a good front. I remember all too well the exception. He had invited me to come to his office at the Elysée. He was at his desk signing the contents of various folders as he was talking to me about the upcoming presidential campaign. Suddenly he got to his feet, and I could see by the look on his face that he was in terrible pain. "Sorry," he said, "it's more than I can cope with."

He always excused himself. I hadn't noticed anything abnormal until he had stood up suddenly, and even the cry of pain was so muffled that I had barely noticed it, since his lips had not even parted. He went over and sprawled on a black leather easy chair. A repressed moan escaped his lips from time to time, but even as he writhed in pain, like a beast being bled, he kept on talking, talking.

"I was counting on living until I died," he said. "But now I'm not sure. The terrible thing about cancer is that there are some days when you lose all desire to live."

"Not you," I protested.

He gave a grimace that was meant to be a smile. "It's true that I do often overcome," he said. "I love life so much that I can't manage to die. That's my whole problem."

He had just belatedly discovered F. Scott Fitzgerald, and said that he found himself identifying with Gatsby. Like Fitzgerald's hero, he was convinced that the future would be bright, but year after year it somehow kept receding, always just beyond his grasp. The future has eluded us again? Not to worry. Tomorrow we'll run even faster, our arms will stretch out even farther. "So we beat on, boats against the current, borne back ceaselessly into the past."

Mitterrand had during the years of his illness a number of doctors whose advice he took or declined, not whimsically but depending on his mood or his physical state. But near the end he dismissed all but one, Dr. Jean-Pierre Tarot, an anesthesiologist and expert in controlling pain. Mitterrand respected him professionally and personally. Once, after Tarot had examined him, near the end, the now former president observed: "When he bends over to examine me, I'm struck by how gentle the expression on his face is. It's as if he were an angel. But I know that he's the angel of death."

On another occasion, as he and Tarot were walking in the Elysée gardens, the president turned to him and said, "Doctor. If you were asked to define me, what would you say?"

"For me," Tarot responded, "you're Machiavelli, Don Corleone, Casanova, and the Little Prince."

"That's pretty good," Mitterrand laughed. "In what proportions?"

"That depends," the doctor said evasively.

"Depends on what?"

"On what time of day you asked me."

From then on, Mitterrand would often ask Tarot: "Right now, who am I, Machiavelli or the Little Prince?"

★

On December 31, 1995, François Mitterrand ate his last meal. This was the traditional Latché New Year's Eve celebration, and he was surrounded by family and friends. He had asked that they serve ortolans, those plump little birds that melt in your mouth. They are a protected species and very rare, but ortolans had been found for him. He ate two, as well as servings of foie gras—both on toast and in slices. Jack Lang, his former minister of culture, held his fork for him. When he took his leave later that evening, his stomach full, he was also taking his leave from the land of the living. He returned to Paris the next morning to die. He didn't die. One day he made up his mind it was all over. He slipped into bed with the idea in mind that he wouldn't get out again, that his next move would be directly from the bed to the coffin. He closed his eyes. Like Clemenceau before him, he refused to see anyone. He asked Dr. Tarot not to give him medicines that would affect his lucidity, no matter what the pain. He also asked Dr. Tarot to field any phone calls that might come in. He was like the German poet Rainer Maria Rilke, who on his deathbed said: "Leave me my own death. I don't want a death by doctors."

He didn't eat. He didn't drink. He waited. Although some family members paid him short visits, his constant companion during his last days was his dog, Baltique. He wanted to dictate his commandments to death the way he always had to the living throughout his life. He meant to live until his death, so that he could watch it come, feel it approach.

He died alive.

NOTES

INTRODUCTION

1. A character in Racine's 1667 tragedy *Andromache,* Hermione has her fiancé Pyrrhus murdered in a jealous rage over his love for Andromache. In a realization of the ease with which love can become hatred, she exclaims, "Can I not know whether I love or hate?"

CHAPTER 1

1. Ninon de Lenclos (1620-1705). A seventeenth-century French woman of letters, whose salon was largely frequented by freethinkers.

CHAPTER 2

1. Louis XIV's death throes went on for a very long time.

2. Aristide Briand (1862-1932). French politician who holds the record for having been named foreign minister no fewer than fifteen times. Between the two world wars, he was a staunch advocate for reconciliation with Germany, and was a signatory to the Pact of Locarno.

3. Édouard Herriot (1872-1957). President of the French parliament from 1936 to 1940, and after the war of the National Assembly from 1947 to 1955. Herriot was also mayor of Lyon for fifty years (1905-1955).

4. Henry IV (1553-1610). King of Navarre (1572-1610) and of France (1589-1610).

5. Jules Mazarin (1602-1661). French prelate and statesman. Italian-born, he became a naturalized French citizen in 1639 and, although never ordained, was named a cardinal after the death of Richelieu.

6. Marie-Jean-Antoine-Nicholas de Caritat (1743-1794), known as the Marquis de Condorcet. French philosopher, mathematician, economist, and statesman. During the years of the French revolution he was arrested as a Girondist and, in prison, committed suicide.

7. Sébastien Le Prestre de Vauban (1633-1707). French marshal, famous for his improving and strengthening the fortifications of French cities in the seventeenth century.

8. Vercingetorix (circa 72-46 B.C.). Gallic general who was named chief of the coalition of Gauls against Caesar in the first century B.C. At first successful, he was later captured and taken to Rome where, after six years of captivity, he was executed.

9. Philip II, or Philip Augustus (1165-1223). King of France (1179-1223).

10. Charles V, "the Wise" (1337-1380). The son of John II, he became king in 1364, after having been regent for eight years. During his reign, he reconquered most of the French provinces the English had previously taken. But sixty years later, the English had reconquered most of France, and it was not until Joan of Arc reawakened French patriotism during Charles VII's rule that, once again, the French expelled the English from their shores—except for Calais, to which the English clung tenaciously.

11. Charles-Maurice de Talleyrand-Périgord (1754-1838). French prelate and diplomat, famous for his cynicism and double-dealing. He served under Napoleon and King Louis-Philippe.

CHAPTER 5

1. Georges Dayan (1915-1979). Mitterrand met Dayan at the end of the 1930s, and he became one of his closest friends and allies. The morning after his election in 1981, Mitterrand paid a visit to his old friend's grave.

2. Jean Riboud (1917-1985). Was chairman of the French conglomerate Schlumberger.

3. A city in the Nièvre region of France and Mitterrand's home base. He was mayor of Château-Chinon from 1959 to 1981.

CHAPTER 6

1. Joseph-Marie de Maistre (1753-1821). French writer and philosopher. His most famous work is *Evenings in St. Petersburg,* published in 1821.

CHAPTER 7

1. After Mitterrand was elected to a second term on May 10, 1988, he named Michel Rocard his prime minister. Three years later, on May 15, 1991, Rocard resigned, or, more accurately, was edged out by François Mitterrand.

2. Edouard Balladur (b. 1929). Chosen as prime minister in 1993 when the conservatives won the elections. It was the second time that President Mitterrand had to govern with an opposition party in legislative power.

3. Jacques Chirac (b. 1932). Then mayor of Paris, who in 1995 was elected president of France, succeeding Mitterrand.

4. Lionel Jospin (b. 1937). For a long time was chairman of the Socialist Party, and was considered Mitterrand's logical successor.

CHAPTER 8

1. Philippe de Haute-Cloque, known as General Leclerc (1902-1947). Marshal of France, he joined General de Gaulle and distinguished himself in the battles of North Africa in World War II. At the head of the French Second Armored Division, he fought in Normandy and in August 1944 liberated Paris from the Germans.

2. On November 1, 1954, shortly after the start of the Algerian insurrection, Mitterrand made that statement in the National Assembly—a political blunder he never lived down.

CHAPTER 9

1. Mitterrand was right. Roughly two years after his death early in 1996 the Socialists, under the leadership of Lionel Jospin, have been voted back into power.

2. Mitterrand's home base. For many years, he represented the region in the French National Assembly.

3. Emile Chartier (1868-1951). French philosopher who wrote under the pen name Alain. His magnum opus, *Propos,* is a cautiously optimistic work emphasizing his belief in the power of thought.

CHAPTER 10

1. A commune in the north of France where, on July 27, 1214, Philip Augustus, with the support of the communes of France, defeated the forces of Emperor Otto IV.

2. Joseph-Ernest Renan (1823-1892). French ecclesiastic and writer, most famous for his *Life of Jesus.*

CHAPTER 12

1. Pierre Drieu la Rochelle (1893-1945). An extreme right-wing writer whose novel *Gilles* marked a generation.

2. Jacques Chardonne (1884-1969). A regional writer originally from Charente, Mitterrand's home turf, and the author most notably of the novel *Claire.*

3. Jules Renard (1864-1910). French novelist and short story writer whose *Journal* provided important insights into the literary life of his time.

4. Octave Mirbeau (1848-1917). French author, a staunch realist like his friend and colleague Jules Renard.

5. Jean-Jacques Rousseau (1712-1778). French writer, composer, and philosopher. His philosophy based itself on his belief that man is essentially good but is corrupted by society, and that a return to "virtuous nature" is necessary. He wrote *The Social Contract* in 1762.

CHAPTER 13

1. One of France's elite schools of higher education.

2. Paul Claudel (1868-1955). French playwright and diplomat, also a deeply religious Catholic.

3. Maurice Barrès (1862-1923). French novelist, journalist, and politician, who as he grew older became increasingly nationalistic.

4. In Roman mythology, Janus was the god of light. He was associated with doors, gates, and all beginnings, and was represented by two faces. His principal temple was near the Roman forum. Its doors were kept open in times of peace, and locked in times of war. Thus Chateaubriand's allusion to Napoleon's deep-rooted desire to constantly make war.

5. Against the advice of his doctors, Mitterrand fulfilled part of his wish. Over the Christmas holidays in 1995 he traveled to Egypt with three close friends and stayed at the Old Cataract Hotel.

CHAPTER 14

1. Mitterrand is viewing history from a Napoleonic viewpoint: at Austerlitz (December 2, 1805) the emperor defeated the armies of Russia and Austria in one of his greatest victories. At Waterloo, of course, ten years later (June 18, 1815), Napoleon suffered his greatest defeat at the hands of the duke of Wellington.